intothefire

To protect the identity of some of the people mentioned in this book, certain names have been changed.

intothe**fire**

jason**marshall**

CanaanPress

CanaanPress

British Library Cataloguing in Publication Data
A record of this book is available from the British Library

ISBN: 978-1-907505-02-7

Book design and typesetting by Andy Ashdown Design
www.andyashdowndesign.co.uk

Cover images © iStockphoto.com

Manufactured in Malta by Gutenberg Press Limited

Contents

ACKNOWLEDGEMENTS

To Dawn – thank you for all your love and unconditional support, for letting me be myself and for allowing me to do the things I do. I don't know where I'd be without you.

To Skyla, Keira and Neave – I love you all; you are all so precious. Thank you for being yourselves.

Life is a story and each one of us are living pages waiting to be read. It is only because of the contributions of others that this is a story worth reading. Thank you to everyone who has walked alongside me, or allowed me to walk alongside them. Thank you to everyone who has clothed, fed, challenged, shaped, loved, laughed, cried and prayed with me over the years.

I also want to say a very big thank you to Lynette, Andy, Steve and especially to Alexa who have helped make this book a reality. I am so grateful for all your encouragement and hard work.

Finally, thank You, Lord Jesus. I just hope this does You justice.

INTRODUCTION

Something In The Way
(Nirvana)

SO THERE I WAS BACK IN BRISTOL. I'd been given a second chance and seemed to have escaped by the skin of my teeth from a pretty dire situation. I signed on at the dole office to look for work and get some benefits to keep me afloat. I had also recently acquired a guitar, which was a helpful distraction. I'd practise scales and noodle around whilst trying to figure out what to do with the newfound freedom that I had. Music was a powerful thing for me. Both then and now. Songs have land marked different eras in my life – the bad and the good. I used to love Nirvana. I could sit for hours listening to their music, learning and playing their songs. Kurt Cobain was my hero.

Unfortunately for me, though, with too much time on my hands, I was soon being drawn into the same old habits that had got me into the mess I'd just escaped from.

Before long, my best mate's girlfriend ended up needing somewhere to stay. I didn't have a problem with the idea. I'd known her for a long time and she was very friendly. We got on really well. I had a spare room in the flat and secretly I fancied her something chronic! I hoped that by helping her out she would end up feeling the same way about me, but of course she didn't. When she moved in, her boyfriend was also over even more than before and we were such a dangerous combination. We would just encourage each other into bad ways. Soon the flat became a little den of booze, drugs, sex and very little else. What began as a chance to get my life straight and back on track – the fresh start people dream about – turned into yet another endless bender.

I was becoming more and more reclusive and paranoid. Soon I would only leave the house to sign on, buy some food and score. That was it – a quick sortie out into the real world then back into my sad little hole. No matter what my circumstances were, I just couldn't shake the desire to get wasted. It swamped me. It dragged me under. I was held down by impossible chains and I couldn't break free. Wherever I was, I always found myself drawn back into the same old, sickening routine.

There seemed to be a constant flow of people through the flat, druggies who ended up sleeping on the floor or the sofa. When I did have space I hated it. I didn't like my own company very much. It made me hurt, so I would drown out the pain with more drug use.

The year was turning out to be far from the new beginning I'd hoped it would be. Just the opposite. I was getting into more of a mess than I could cope with, and I soon realised that no matter how hard you try to change, there are some things that weigh you down to the point where life can seem hopeless. Futile. I could move house, set up somewhere new, change the outward appearances, do all of that, but I couldn't solve my biggest problem – me. I was bad tempered and irritable, angry and aggressive. I was on a constant mission to find a steady supply of gear. Insecure and desperate, I hated what I was turning into, but there didn't seem to be a thing I could do about it. I was an addict and I simply couldn't stop.

So was this it for me? Was this all there would ever be? After all, if you stripped away the drugs and the music, what was left?

If ever I needed a way out, it was now.

1

Little Child
(The Beatles)

IT'S BEEN SAID THAT EVERYONE has a book inside them; at the very least each one of us has a story to tell. When I first started writing, all I wanted was to share what's happened to me. But I've come to realise that it's not just about *my* story; it's about encouraging others to share their stories too, whether by writing them in a book, or just by spending time with people and talking to them. Our stories have weight. They have significance. Yet, in our culture, we've lost the art of story-telling. We rely on the media for our entertainment, and it tells us the stories that it wants us to hear – though many of the values that it carries might not be those we would agree with or want to encourage.

So much of the ancient world was founded on a tradition of sharing stories, handing tales down from generation to generation. My hope is that in sharing my story with you, it will encourage you to share yours, no matter how simple or how spectacular. If it's a God story it needs to be heard. The world is hungry for God stories to be told, and it's time for us to stand up and share what our loving God has done for us. Our God loves us and loves it when we speak of Him and share the reality of our faith with others because He loves them, too. He has commissioned us to share that love with the world around us.

For many, the thought of telling their story is challenging. It's easy to think, 'But I don't have a testimony like yours,' or, 'I've always known God – I grew up in a Christian home. I've always known God's provision, but nothing exciting has happened to me.' Yet the truth is that, to a lost world that doesn't even believe there is a God, any story that speaks of His love, His grace, His healing, His provision, His teaching and His involvement in our lives is a revelation. It's what the world needs to hear – that God is real; He is alive and well and He wants people to know it. And it's up to us to share that. We are to be salt shakers and light bearers to a world in need of God's love.

I am currently in my thirties, husband to Dawn and father of three beautiful girls, Skyla Faith, Keira Grace and Neave Hope. Over the years I've worked for churches and voluntary organisations; I've earned a living painting and decorating; I've served in shops and in pubs, and I've paid my way being a musician and guitar tutor.

I am also a follower of Jesus. And in 2008, I had a dream; a dream that turned a normal year on its head.

It started out as most years do; New Year's Eve with a few

friends and a couple of beers; the odd event pencilled in and a summer holiday in France booked early. Other than that a very ordinary-looking 12 months lined up. But God, as He so often does, had other ideas.

The recent course of events all started in April 2008 at Spring Harvest, a Christian convention held over three weeks around Easter in two separate venues in the UK. I'd been asked to help lead the family worship event in Minehead. It's a few hours a day of fun, music, short talks, puppets and stories. The week was going well. My friend, Steve, was leading the team, and the rest of us were all doing our bit. I was heading up the band.

One night in my chalet, I was woken by a vivid dream: I was standing in a garden with a few others. We saw the glory of God and heard the words, 'He knew you had a gift and didn't want you to miss out or not use it as you have a habit of doing'. There are a few other details, but this was the part that really got my attention. I woke up instantaneously filled with a sense of awe.

The next morning I mentioned the dream to a few friends. To them, it felt like the 'passing on of a mantle', as in the story of Elijah and Elisha in the Bible.

If I'm honest, I was more than a little unsure about what that was supposed to mean. After all who was I? I'm just an ordinary guy, trying his best to walk with God, and wanting to help others know Him, too. So I got up and got on with the events at Spring Harvest. We had a great team and we laughed a lot. Then at the end of our week, we went home.

But once back there, I spoke to a few more friends who had been exploring the way God speaks through dreams, and they felt that my dream was truly significant. Again, mantles were mentioned, but not just in terms of myself – for everyone.

That's when I started to ask questions: 'So what are You saying, Lord? What do You want from me?'

I continued seeking God, praying, fasting, digging in.

Little did I know that this would set in motion a whole host of events and circumstances that would literally change my heart and the direction of my life …

That life began for me on 11 March 1974. I was born to hippie parents, the middle child of three, with an older sister and a younger brother. My mum and dad had met at a youth drop-in centre during the late 1960s and were a big part of hippie culture. Later on they got involved in the emerging folk music scene. Mum came from a Methodist family, the elder of two. She has always been very intelligent, kind, hospitable and bubbly, though I don't think she really connected with the lifestyle that my grandparents represented. I always got the impression she found it restricting and stifling. Subsequently she rebelled against the strict religious background, falling pregnant at an early age with my older sister, Sara. She married my father in her late teens – possibly not the future she was dreaming of.

Dad grew up in an average working class family in Bristol, the younger of two. He was bright like my mum, and came from a family of engineers and shipwrights. When he was only in his early teens, his own father died and, as far as I can gather, from there on my dad became something of a rebel. I don't know that much about his early years, but from what I've gleaned he had quite a colourful background. He was involved in the biker scene and had an interesting relationship with drugs and drink. I found out later that he'd had several brushes with the law over the years.

Mum told me that when she first met Dad he was living with his mother. He had moved out of home on and off but he always ended up back there when the money ran out. He was a very charismatic man, and Mum was flattered by his attention – perhaps particularly as she was so unhappy at school where she'd been bullied and felt she didn't fit in. When she was with Dad and his friends, she was among people who didn't appear to judge. She felt accepted by them – hell's angels, druggies, dossers, and kids who were alienated from society, just as she was.

I didn't learn much of this until much later in my life. In the society of the time, you didn't air your laundry in public, or even within your own four walls it seemed. That said, given the way I looked up to Dad, I'm pretty glad I didn't know too much about his past back then.

My memories of my early years are sketchy to say the least. We lived in quite an old house in a small village called Mangotsfield outside Bristol. It wasn't much and needed a lot of work doing to it. My parents didn't have a great deal of money at the time. Dad was training as a teacher, and there was only his grant to live on. Mum learned to manage and became a very astute shopper. We didn't really see much of Dad, I suppose, and in any case, he was getting frustrated by the restrictions of a young family.

The house was what you might call a 'doer-upper'. I can recall some bare, plastered walls, and a galley-style kitchen, small but enough for us. There was a through-lounge with a large fish tank and an open fire, and a black and white TV in one corner. We had a little, narrow garden but the bottom was overgrown and full of brambles. Even so, there was a patch of lawn to play on and a slide. Mum once told me that, when I was born, the house was in such a state that the hospital wouldn't let her take me home. We ended up living with Nan Marshall – Dad's mum – until Simon (my younger brother) was born.

Simon and I shared a room. We used to mess around in there. We'd spend ages jumping off the shelves of the corner airing cupboard onto Simon's bed. We were full of energy, always climbing stuff, play-fighting, leaping off things and occasionally biting each other! One of our favourite stunts was to jump down the stairs from as high up as we dared onto piles of cushions. We'd get up to all sorts of craziness like that, finding ways to entertain ourselves, always up to mischief.

A lot of our time was spent at my Nan Marshall's house in Kingswood. She had a lovely home and it always felt light and safe there. We had space to play in the garden and there was a swing; but mostly what we all really enjoyed was being around Nan. She would spoil us. Many a weekend was spent there, and family roast dinner on a Sunday was a real treat. We'd be there most Christmases, too. In fact the majority of my positive childhood memories have come from being around

Nan. As we grew up, we were all especially fond of her toast and Marmite – massive toast doorsteps of fresh cut bread, smothered in butter and generous helpings of the 'love it or hate it' spread. It was so good.

All three of us went to the nearby play school, although I hated being left there. In fact, I really didn't like going at all. When we were old enough, we moved on to the local primary school, just over the road from our house. I remember how we'd say hello to the crossing lady, who would occasionally give us sweets …

It all sounds very normal, I guess, and I suppose it was; a normal childhood – certainly a far better start in life than some have had.

But that was on the surface.

It was underneath where things didn't look nearly as good.

2

Communication Breakdown

(Led Zeppelin)

IF I'M HONEST, I CAN PROBABLY COUNT on the fingers of one hand the really positive memories I have of early family life.

And barely any of them include Dad.

I do remember one Christmas when he got into a Santa outfit. Once he even dressed up as Miss Piggy for a school fancy dress event, and there was another time when we had some friends over and I remember him doing a few mind reading tricks. He had Mum telling him what was going on from behind our backs but we couldn't figure it out; I was completely baffled. There were also times when Dad and I would play together, bundling and stuff on the floor. He'd lift me up and throw me about, the normal kind of father-and-son rough and tumble. One time we went fishing and I caught a minnow. I was so proud. There's even a photo to prove it somewhere. Then there was the time I had a new football kit for my birthday. These were all good memories but, to be honest, sometimes I think they're only in my head because of the photos I've seen.

I'm told I was happy enough as a boy but most of what I can remember has a negative vibe to it. Mum and Dad were always fighting for a start. I would regularly sit at the top of the stairs listening, crying, worrying; I was always a sensitive kid. Dad was very quick to lose his temper and Mum was certainly not happy. Constant fighting, screaming and shouting seemed to be a regular backdrop to our family life.

Mum told me it was like living on a knife-edge. She never knew what mood Dad would be in. Even if she said something relatively non-controversial, she could end up being hit. She usually only challenged him if he did anything to hurt us children, and would often hide the bad things we had done from him to protect us. What she tried to do was keep him happy – keep the peace – which meant pretty much letting him do whatever he wanted. Mum often didn't know where he was, or when he'd be home, yet he always expected her to be around and available.

Because there was never much money, Mum had a hard time feeding and clothing us. In fact, if it hadn't have been for Nan, we wouldn't even have had decent shoes. Dad still managed to go out drinking, though, and to buy the things that he wanted. Mum used to make most of our clothes, or she got them from second hand sales. She was very good at managing on a tight budget.

It wasn't just Mum who got hit. There were times when I was

on the receiving end of Dad's aggression, too, and I'm sure I wasn't the only one of us kids it happened to. One time that sticks in my mind was being slapped hard round the face at the dinner table for saying or doing something that Dad considered out of order. I had what felt like a huge handprint across my cheek. It stung, and I remember going to school feeling as though everyone could see it. Talk about self-conscious. I felt really stupid and embarrassed.

There certainly wasn't much security there for a small kid to hold on to. I used to sing and rock myself to sleep regularly. I cried a lot. I know I was sad and probably anxious. I also used to have a recurring dream: heavy clouds, sepia in colour, rolling in over me. They'd leave me with a sense of heaviness and oppression. Maybe I was picking up on what was to come – I knew things at home were far from right – but what followed next really did knock me sideways.

I was only six years old when it happened. After all that fighting, screaming, shouting and tension, my parents split. I remember having the conversation with Dad. He came into my room, told me he was leaving and said goodbye. From then on, that was that; it was just Mum and us three kids.

I discovered much later that, despite Mum's unhappiness, it wasn't a joint decision. She was as shocked as we were when he came home one day and announced that he was leaving to be with someone else. It hit Mum for six, too. She'd been with him since she was 16. She'd given up what was left of her childhood to be with him. Then, all of a sudden, in his eyes, she was past it. And she was only about 26.

For me, the feeling of abandonment and rejection dug in

deep. I felt terrible. I thought that somehow I was to blame, that I wasn't good enough. I had failed. I was just so young and I didn't have the means to process this mixed bag of emotions churning inside me. The pain was horrible.

I remember crying with Mum on the sofa the day Dad left. But from then on, it was something we never talked about. We never really talked about much in our family. I think there were so many raw nerves, most things were best avoided.

I suppose that's when things began to change for me. That was the time my life started to take a new direction. An empty sadness quickly settled in, and quite possibly the beginnings of depression, too.

We went to visit my grandparents (Mum's mum and dad) that summer in Devon. My nan was aware that I wasn't happy. I seemed to have gone from being a fairly normal and lively kid to an introverted, sad, angry little boy who wanted to be left alone. But Nan was kind and would help me find things to occupy me, like doing the dishes, peeling potatoes and polishing shoes – simple things, I know, but I learnt to do them and do them well. I've always been good at using my hands.

It was during that summer that I found a copy of *Joseph and his Amazing Technicolor Dreamcoat* in my Grandad's music collection. I listened to it over and over, letting myself escape into the story. I guess it kept me from feeling the pain. Only as it turned out, it wasn't really a good thing. Of course I'd never have realised at the time, but this was the beginnings of an unhelpful coping mechanism just waiting to consume me.

I didn't really have any idea back then how all this was affecting my brother and sister. It wasn't something I thought about. I was clearly in pain, and I guess they were, too. But, as I said, we weren't a family that talked to each other, and I think I must have just shut everything out. It was my way of dealing with it. I really didn't know what else to do, not that I remember making any conscious decisions. It would be decades before I felt free from the hurt of all that rejection.

Despite how things were at home when Dad was there, in my own way, I think I had idolised him. When he left, my understanding was so limited that I ended up making some very bad assumptions: I was to blame for everything; I'd fallen short.

It was this way of thinking that paved the way for years of striving desperately for approval – only, as it turned out, it was an empty striving that was later to come back and sting me. I missed my dad and always felt that his abandonment had left a gaping hole in my heart. I was desperate to show him that I was good enough. I suppose what I was really hoping for was that maybe he'd come back – if not to stay then at least to take me away with him.

I found myself wanting to be at Nan Marshall's most of the time. It was a safe place – secure and stable. I remember one time being so sad that I had to go home after spending the weekend at her house that I was actually in tears as I walked up the path to our front door.

Not too long after my parents' split, we moved to a smaller, rented house on a busy main road in a nearby town. Mum and Dad had borrowed money from some friends to buy our home, but everything had gone wrong. Dad had employed people he knew to do the building work on our new extension, but they made such a mess of it that it had to be demolished.

That used up most of the money and the work was never finished. Meantime, the old part of the house was in a really bad state with damp and rot. It needed a fortune spending on it to make it habitable. Mum was really struggling to keep it warm. When Dad left, he said he would pay the mortgage but that was all – so Mum had no extra income to do any of the repairs. Originally she tried to get a council house, but the council said that, as we already had somewhere to live, they couldn't help. The only way out was to sell the house, rent somewhere, and claim benefits, which for Mum was horribly degrading. She even had to use our Post Office savings – money put by for her kids – to try and help make ends meet.

We changed schools, too, which was supposed to make life happier – easier. I was being bullied at the primary school where we lived before. The change didn't really help, though. I guess at least I knew my bullies back at the old school. After all, I'd grown up round them, and I did have a few friends, too. Now I was somewhere different, the new kid with no friends and new issues to contend with. My entire life felt out of control.

I realise now that it really wasn't just us kids who were suffering through all of this. The whole thing was incredibly hard on Mum, too. At the time, though, all I could think about was what was happening to me.

It was around then that I started playing up.

3

Under Pressure
(Queen & David Bowie)

MUM WAS TRYING TO GET HER LIFE BACK ON TRACK. It must have been so difficult for her – three kids, no income, and she had started studying for a degree. Yet she seemed to be so angry all the time. She would shout at me and she could get really threatening. Sometimes she would lose it so badly.

And I was starting to cause trouble for her. I didn't want to go to school. I hated it. I felt unsafe and vulnerable and would try almost every trick in the book to avoid going. Sometimes I'd get really sick, partly out of anxiety, but at other times I'd fake it. The bottom line was I was insecure and scared, lonely, angry and very, very sad. I think I must have pushed Mum away. I couldn't let her get close to me. I was starting to get violent, too, and she was beginning to realise she didn't know how to deal with me.

I didn't have many friends back then, so I started finding ways to amuse myself on my own. One day, to pass the time,

I figured it would be a laugh to throw stones across the road at passing cars. I would lob a stone and duck down behind the hedge. Of course, that didn't last long. A guy whose car I hit pulled up and came to the house. Mum was furious and threatened to kill me. That was bad. I thought I was well and truly for it. She really scared me that day.

With my behaviour getting worse, I think Mum was finding it difficult to cope. At times she would just lash out at me, sometimes threatening to have me sent into care. She could come out with some really hurtful things, often saying, 'You're just like your Dad.' *Well, that's great*, I'd end up thinking. *You hated Dad, and that's why he left. You wished he was dead, so if I'm like him, that must be what you want for me too. Great. Thanks.*

Mum did try very hard to make things better. 'You said you wanted to live with your dad,' she has told me since, 'and I asked him on numerous occasions if you could live with him, but he didn't even have you to stay more than once. He used all sorts of excuses – children need to be with their mother; the three of you shouldn't be split up, all of that.'

It's amazing just how powerful words can be. I know Mum didn't really want me dead. I know that I wasn't truly *like* my dad. Just because I have character traits like him, that doesn't mean I am him. But Mum was finding life tough and I guess some of her struggling was just coming out at me. We've all heard the saying, 'Sticks and stones will break my bones but words will never harm me'. But that is so untrue. Back then, the words that were spoken to me just continued to reinforce my new belief system: that I was no good; no one wanted or loved me; that I was rubbish.

As time went on, Mum had a few boyfriends. One of them was very kind, I remember. He had a nice house and wrote books. I really liked him and hoped that he might be around for a bit, but the relationship didn't seem to go anywhere. I found out later he was just a kind friend.

There was another who was a big, scary, bearded guy and he terrified me. One time, I must have done something wrong – I'd probably been rude to Mum – and the next thing I remember was him dragging me up the stairs by one arm like a rag doll. I felt utterly powerless and I was really scared. Mum told me that after that, she ended the relationship, but the fear and the pain had still found their way in.

Despite everything, Mum really did want the best for us. Some of the circumstances we'd ended up in were beyond her control, but that didn't stop them leaving scars. After a while, things mount up. All these incidents were twisting me up inside, paving the way for attitude issues towards those in authority, and an inability to trust anyone. It makes you realise just how fragile we are as human beings.

Mum has told me since that she did try to explain all that was going on, but she couldn't get through to me. My sister was older and able to understand things better and come to terms with them, and my brother was so young he didn't really know Dad because he was never around. Somehow for me, though, the hurt and damage I was feeling was just too much for me to process.

A good friend of mine says that we don't remember days, only moments. When I look back over those early years, that's been so true. Sadly, what I seem to have is memory upon memory of negative moments. I can see so clearly where lies, fear, insecurity and rejection have got sown into my life. We are products of what we believe about ourselves and if we're brought up around negativity, we're going to reap that in our lives.

Eventually my mum and now stepdad, Ian, got together. They were friends from a long while back. They used to play in a folk band together and I remember thinking how nice he was. I've grown to value him so much over the years. He's amazing and has always stood by my mum and the three of us kids, too. What a man, to take on three children, one of whom was me (I was turning out to be not so nice around then), just so that he could be with Mum. Apparently Nan even asked him at one point, 'Are you sure you know what you're doing?' His reply was simply, 'I love Mo' (Mum's nick name). What a statement.

Sadly, though, I was hurting, and found it too hard to let him get close to me.

Mum and Ian got married when I was about ten years old. We moved again to another new house in a village called Frampton, all ready for a fresh start. I began going to yet another school, but at least it was better than the last one, and I soon made a couple of friends. I even managed to gain a little self-respect by putting one of the school bullies on his butt in a playground scuffle.

Our new street was full of kids my age. I suppose there was an average of two children per household in a cul-de-sac of around 40 houses. Even so, it was taking me a long time to feel as though I was part of the crowd, so I started stealing. I would take money to buy sweets, then use the sweets to win friends. I stole mainly from Mum and Ian's wallets, pockets and purses, but I'd also take any other money I found around the house. I was always on the lookout for money, much to my parents' frustration.

This habit of stealing kept growing, and as I got older I would often shoplift. I'd take anything I could fit easily in my hand, pocket or school bag; it became quite a fun distraction.

My brother and sister seemed to settle into out new way of life better than I did to start with, but eventually I did find my feet and we'd all knock around together. There was a lot of laughter and some really good times with the kids in that road. We had plenty of silly adventures – going for river hikes, playing knock out ginger, garden hopping, and forever riding our bikes.

During the holidays or at weekends when we weren't staying at Nan Marshall's, we would get dragged around to folk festivals all over the place. Mum and Ian were always buzzing off somewhere. For us kids (well, mainly my brother and me), these festivals were boring with a capital B. My sister enjoyed the Céilidh and Morris Dancing, but Simon and I would just wander around trying to find ways of occupying ourselves.

Having said that, one year I met up with a group of performers who juggled, uni-cycled, did illusions and escape routines, and for the first time in my life, I felt inspired. Before too long, I was juggling and learning circus skills, and I loved it. I juggled all the time – in the garden, at school, everywhere. For years after that I would dream of running away to join the circus.

About the same time, my parents decided to buy a camper van. The first one was a white Fiat conversion which was pretty flimsy. In fact the day we collected it, Ian snapped the key in the ignition lock. Then, on the way home, sadly we hit a huge dog and smashed the front of the van right in. It literally had a v-shaped dent in it with the remains of the poor dog attached to the underneath for some time to come. I'm not sure that we kept it for long.

Our second van was a VW camper, which was really cool when it worked – at least, we all thought so. My brother and I occasionally slept out in it for fun, and when it broke down, I used to enjoy helping Ian to fix it. I reckon I could still remove and rebuild the engine bay, we took it apart so often.

However, all my street friends just found it an excuse to take the mickey. By now I had had several run-ins with different kids in the road. I tended to get laughed at quite regularly, usually because I wasn't as good at doing the kind of things they did. One particular time I was being teased for something and I lost my temper. I started throwing stones and anything else I could grab at this group of kids to 'warn them off'. I suppose this might have helped had my aim been any good. As it was, I was an awful shot. I couldn't hit the side of a barn at 20 paces. So that angry moment (desperately serious back then, although now it seems so funny) didn't do me any good at all in the credibility stakes.

Unfortunately, the VW wasn't the only laughing point for the other kids on the street. They knew about my parents' folk obsession, and, embarrassingly, they had also discovered that Morris Dancing was one of Mum and Ian's pastimes. All this added up to being just plain weird. To them, the folk scene was all about hippies and flower power. It led to me being nicknamed 'Flower' for at least the next five years of my life.

Despite the fallouts, things did start to settle down for a while.

I had a group of mates, and was going to the local scout group, but I still didn't enjoy school. The pain I felt was always there, bubbling under the surface. As I got older and the confusion of my emotions began to collide with teenage hormones, there were more and more clashes, some of which started to get violent. I would frequently lash out. I'd smash, kick and punch things. Never mind that they were important or that I really liked them, I just couldn't control my temper.

The bulk of my anger was aimed at Ian. It wasn't really him I was angry with, I was just so hurt and lost. The anger became a defence and controlling mechanism. The problem was that it was exploding all over the place. I was becoming uncontrollable. Ian seemed to bear the brunt of it and, in retrospect, I think if he hadn't been around much of that fury would have been targeted at Mum.

I remember on one occasion completely losing it and kicking one of our newly fitted kitchen cupboard doors, which just fell apart. Another time I punched a hole through one of the doors in the house. I felt awful but I couldn't keep a lid on it. It was either smash up an object, or hurt someone – or myself. Once I got so totally out of control that Ian literally had to sit on me to get me to calm down.

But I was getting bigger and stronger, and anger was erupting all the time. When I think of what could have happened if I'd let it all out at Mum, it's a little scary. I can't imagine what sort of damage I could have done if I'd started targeting people instead of things. It was clear that I was out of control, and both Mum and Ian were finding it hard to deal with.

No doubt about it, I was heading for trouble.

4

Light My Fire
(The Doors)

MUM MIGHT HAVE MOVED ON IN HER LIFE WITH IAN, but Dad was still around. He had a new girlfriend and I got on well with her. Nan would have us to stay with her at weekends and the two of them would come and have Sunday dinner with us, though seeing them together seemed to make my feelings of rejection worse. I couldn't understand why he didn't want to have me around with him, too. I wasn't interested in seeing him for just a couple of hours. I wanted and needed him more than that – his time and his attention. I think in retrospect it might have been easier if, after he left, I'd never seen him again, because each time I did, it gave me a glimmer of hope: maybe things would change and I could go and live with him … but it never happened.

There was one great thing that did happen during the early years at Frampton. My little sister, Fiona, was born. She was wonderful – born at home, and barely a few hours old when

I first saw her. I fell in love with this little bundle. As she got older, she became a fun distraction, taking me away from how I was feeling. My brother and I would spend hours playing games with her, helping Mum with her, and we would often end up laughing till we ached. Fiona's always been very special to me.

However, even with her arrival, I still went on getting harder and harder for my mum and stepdad to control. I couldn't 'let anyone in', and even though Ian was a good guy, whenever we started to get close, I'd end up reacting and pushing him away. As a family we went through counselling, but all that seemed to do was upset everyone. I also had a school shrink, who never really did any good. I'm not even sure how many times I saw him. Nothing was helping. The only certain thing was that I wasn't getting any better.

By now I was in secondary school – and once again, I didn't like it. On the first day I got into a fight with one of the kids in my class, and after that I found myself continuing to get into trouble off and on. It's not that I was a bad kid as such, I just didn't like the whole school environment, and I was hardly the most secure of children. I found there were maybe a few subjects and teachers I got on with, but really that was about it. I was so unhappy I'd often pretend to be ill.

I remember once being called out of a science lesson to the Deputy Head's office, where I was to meet the shrink.

'Why are you here?' the Deputy asked me.

'I don't know,' I replied.

I mean, I really didn't. We never talked about things at home, so I didn't have a clue that I was supposed to be seeing this

31

guy. It was a complete surprise to me. The Deputy Head didn't believe me. She pretty much called me a liar to my face.

This was just one of several occasions when I was accused of something I either didn't know about or didn't do. Several accusations came from close friends who blamed me for stealing from them or doing something else I hadn't; or they came from authority figures reacting prematurely over something that was nothing to do with me. Things like that cut deep. The ground was ripe for more feelings of rejection, and that particular moment with the Deputy Head really hurt.

I honestly couldn't make out what was going on. I was a mess. I didn't have a handle on why I was behaving the way I was. It wasn't as if I had chosen what was happening in my life. The incident with the school Deputy just added fuel to the fire. I really started to hate the place; to hate any authority figure in my life. I began to bunk off as much as possible. I just wanted to stay home; in bed or in my room. I guess it was the only place I felt safe. I think there were weeks when I only went in three days out of five, if I went in at all.

One outlet for me was scouts. I used to enjoy getting away from home and just hanging out, doing guy stuff, learning to cook, tie knots, canoeing, lighting fires, and camping, all the usual scout activities. I was thriving there. I loved it and really looked forward to the camping and hiking trips.

Another form of release was weight lifting, the Olympic kind – not body building but the sort of thing they do for competitions. I started going to the local gym when I was about 14 years old. I teamed up with a couple of guys from my street who were doing it, too. Even though I was the youngest there, I really enjoyed it. Soon I was filling out and getting even stronger. I did start doing some competitions but unfortunately had to stop when I began to get a lot of pain in my knees.

It was around this time that I discovered porn. All my mates were showing me stuff, not to mention the magazines I'd found myself. Soon enough, I'd developed a lovely little existence of porn, masturbation, stealing and bunking off school. What a charming young man I was turning into … NOT.

I may not have known God when I was growing up but, as I look back over these early years now, I can see that, through all the sadness and negativity, even then He was teaching me lessons that I know will stay with me for the rest of my life. During my time as a scout, the biggest fascination to me was fire. I loved it – the way it captivates you and draws you in as you watch the flames dance and curl, flickering with a life of their own. I loved the heat and the smell.

Even as a young kid I was always entranced by it. We had a large open fire in the lounge of our first house, and it was always great fun sitting around it, watching things burn and cooking toast by it. You'd feel the heat from the flames and hear the noise of the wood popping. I remember being told off after playing with matches and consequently burning holes in the carpet behind the armchair in the lounge (I know I got in pretty major trouble with Dad over that one). As I got older, my brother and I would often be found lighting fires or playing with matches. I suppose some of it was down to a natural sense of curiosity, but for me the lessons seemed to go much deeper.

I'm intrigued by the way fire consumes. Whatever goes near it gets burned; there's very little that can stop that. As more fuel is drawn in, the hotter the flames get.

Fire is dangerous, too. There's no denying that playing with it isn't safe. Yet it's also life giving. Too close and you get burned, but too far away and you get cold.

These days, I often think of God as a fire. He's white hot. As you get drawn towards Him, He captivates, enthrals – just as a moth gets drawn to a light. Then He consumes you and your attention. He's not tame or controllable, and most definitely not predictable, yet when you're away from Him you go cold, and when you draw near, there's life.

I still love lighting fires. I enjoy making a bonfire or burning old, private papers – I really don't need much of an excuse to have one. I often think in another life I might have been a pyromaniac!

However, what I find I love the most are the lessons I've learned. I love meeting people who are like dry kindling, hungry and ready to be set on fire for God. I love it when they grasp the love of God for themselves and then get utterly consumed by Him. There's no denying that God can completely turn your world upside down. He is God after all, yet He can be totally trusted. If He says it's time to throw something to the flames, He knows it'll be for our benefit.

I want to be on fire.

I want to light fires.

5

Sex & Drugs
& Rock & Roll

(Ian Dury and the Blockheads)

IT WAS WHEN I WAS ABOUT 15 YEARS OLD and went on scout camp to Holland that I discovered booze for the first time – and it was legal. Boy, did I drink. I got so hammered. I remember having to lean against the wall to hold myself up. The room was spinning. I was finding everything ridiculously funny, walking about in crooked lines and generally feeling euphoric. Soon I hadn't a clue what I was doing, eventually throwing my guts up at the end of the evening. Even the historic hangover, which I can still remember to this day, wasn't enough to put me off. I already had the beginnings of an addictive personality developing.

After that experience I just kept at it, getting drunk on Friday nights, sneaking in the pub with my older mates. Then I started smoking, too. To start with it was just for the buzz but soon I was smoking regularly.

Amazingly, I had managed to get through school, though didn't do too well with exams. Then I landed an apprenticeship with an aero engineering company in my hometown, but at the same time, my stepdad's work changed and my parents needed to move to Derby. Though I probably could have moved my apprenticeship to go with them, everyone I cared about, most notably my nan, was still in Bristol, so I stayed there with her. We redecorated the old boys' room and I was soon settled in. The strange thing was that, even though it was my choice to stay, somehow I still felt the sting of rejection when my parents moved north.

The first months of my apprenticeship went well. I was 16, I'd got myself a new motorcycle, I had money. I was finally cool (at least I thought so). I was hanging out with my friends and having some fun. I was enjoying the job. I liked the learning environment, and even though at the weekends I would go out drinking and smoking, on the whole I started to thrive.

Of course, I didn't realise it at the time but that was simply the calm before the storm. If I thought I'd climbed out of one hole, there was an even deeper pit lying there, just waiting for me to stumble blindly into it.

I was happy with my work for a while. I loved the challenge and getting to know new people. But as I was so desperate to fit in I found myself hanging out with the rebels. A lot of the guys at college were doing drugs. To start off with they would smoke a bit of pot, usually just on college days when we were in a classroom all day. It was clear they weren't taking the college work seriously and, from my perspective, they seemed to be having a lot of fun. Inevitably it wasn't long before I was joining them.

It all started when we went on a team-building trip to a theme park in the Midlands. The pot heads were usually hanging around together and at this point I had no idea what smoking pot was all about. I'd managed to arrive at this point in my life still pretty sheltered all things considered. I didn't even know what it was until that day.

Sometime during the morning I was introduced to my first taste of cannabis. We snuck into a little den in the woods and someone brought out a pipe, filled it with hash, passed it around – and hey presto! I had never laughed so much. At times I thought I was going to pass out. The whole day whizzed by. For someone so sad, lonely and depressed, this was an unbelievable experience. Seriously, I must have giggled for the whole day. I was so high and I loved it. Almost immediately I was hooked. From then on whenever I could, I was set on getting high.

College on a Friday was a great excuse to get wasted. We would only have to sit in a classroom and make notes, so at lunch we'd go outside and get high. Afterwards, back in the classroom, I would almost be passed out on my desk with a pile of munchies stacked up next to me, but somehow I managed to get away with it. I even did well with the exams that year.

However, it wasn't long before I was getting stoned most evenings, too. To start off with it was a social thing, but very quickly I'd be smoking a joint on arrival at work, in my breaks, on my own. As I spent more and more time with my druggie mates, that became the focus of my spare time. I ended up regularly disappearing to the garage at the back of Nan's house to 'work on my motorbike' and basically get wrecked! The addiction was setting in.

I'm amazed that I never got myself into serious trouble when working with heavy machinery. There were days when I would be working at the lathes or milling machines – big, metal-munching tools – and I was so stoned I'd be falling asleep whilst operating them. All it would have taken was one slip and I would have been dragged into the machine and, quite literally, turned into minced meat!

Hanging around with this new crowd was fun, and it wasn't just drugs they opened my eyes to. They introduced me to clubbing. I'm not talking your average beer and dance clubs, but dark rock clubs where we would go to hit on girls (I was never very good at that), get high and score more drugs (I was *very* good at that). We'd do lines of speed in the toilets and get stoned. We'd often drink till we ran out of money. Then we'd have to walk home (about four miles) because there'd be no bus fare left.

I was changing. In fact, little by little, I was sinking. My music taste got heavier, my clothing got crustier, my hair got longer, and I just stopped taking care of myself. I started getting piercings. At the time they were still relatively unusual and would draw some interesting looks from people. Eventually all my money was going on drugs, booze, music or running my motorbike. I started experimenting with drugs, too, trying LSD and magic mushrooms.

I had not long turned 17 when I met a girl. My parents and sisters were still doing the folk scene and I had gone over to a festival to see them. It was relatively near home and was an excuse to get out on the road. By now I had a bigger motorbike and grabbed every opportunity I could to take it out for a ride.

Not long after I got there, I met up with my older sister and her mates. At this point I was Sara's cool younger brother – a bit different, usually stoned and always rebellious. I soon got to know all Sara's mates, and within that group was a girl called Laura. We spent most of the weekend flirting and hanging out together. She was so pretty and fun to be around, and she took a real interest in me. From very early on, I found myself hooked on her, too. She was a bit older than I was, but she showed me acceptance and intimacy, and I fell head over heels for her.

It was weird, but I seemed to have gone from being the goofy, odd little kid to the guy with the bike, the long hair, the leather jacket and some money – and very quickly I became popular to be around. Now, instead of using money to buy sweets and make friends like I did when I was younger, I found drugs were a good way to get to know people. I was also developing an uncanny ability to bump into other druggies. Everywhere I went, I'd meet up with pot heads.

When the festival ended and I went home, I couldn't keep this girl out of my mind. I was obsessed. She was all I could think about. I wrote to her and we planned to meet up at another festival later in the year. College was going all right. I was getting high most of the time, but I had a focus. I carried on earning money and hanging out with my mates, but I was really pining for Laura.

Eventually we did meet up again. Our relationship began to develop and, before I knew it, we were together. I was in love, and Laura moved to university on the south coast.

For a while things seemed to settle into some kind of routine. We would travel up and down the country to visit each other, although we kept things laid back and relaxed. But it wasn't long before the high of feeling in love was beginning to wear a bit thin for me. I soon met a local girl and, of course, I figured, why not have a girlfriend in each town? So that's what I did. During the week I'd be with one girl and then at the weekend I'd see the other.

In the middle of this crazy love thing I had going on, I was doing quite a lot of drugs, still disappearing to Nan's garage to get high.

One day Dad came by to visit. I can remember it so clearly. I came in from the garage. I was always pleased to see my dad. He'd pop in occasionally and, as I was living at his mum's house, I was ending up seeing him more regularly than ever before.

Dad sussed that I'd been smoking dope. Being no stranger to the stuff himself, I guess he spotted the signs. I mean, it was obvious really. There I was, smiling and laughing like an idiot, with bloodshot eyes and a stupid look on my face, caned out of my head.

I think he may have had a conversation with Nan about things. I'd been having friends over, doing drugs and smoking in my room, then burning incense to cover up the smell. Basically I was being totally disrespectful to Nan. I think she'd cottoned on to the fact that I was up to no good. Sadly, she was also seeing history repeat itself with my behaviour and some of the things my dad had got up to a long time before.

When Dad finally left the house, I went to see him off.

And that was the moment.

That was the instant that sent me off to druggie heaven.

My dad leaned over, put his hand on my shoulder and, rather than give me a lecture or punish me, he simply said, 'Jase, I don't mind you doing dope. Just don't do it around your nan or in the house. OK?'

That was probably the greatest pat on the back I'd ever had from my dad. My search for approval had finally come back to sting me. Right there and then. I felt as if Dad had pretty much told me that what I was doing was fine. 'Just be smart and don't get caught.'

Suddenly, I felt great. Actually, I felt invincible. Something inside me went, 'Dad says it's OK, so it's OK. Who's going to convince me otherwise?' It was as though finally, after so many years, my dad was approving of my behaviour. It was illegal, but I didn't care.

I had *my dad's approval* – and that's what I'd longed for all my life.

6

Big Trouble
(David Lee Roth)

AT AROUND THE TIME of that bizarrely momentous occasion with my dad, a group of us from college decided we would club together and buy a large amount of dope. It would be cheaper for all of us if we did it that way. However, fortunately for me as it turned out, things didn't go according to plan.

The idea was for one of the guys in the group to arrange with his dealer that we would drive into town, grab some gear and get back before the lunch buzzer rang.

The day before the big deal, I was on my way home from my girlfriend's in Bristol when I got the 'munchies'. I was stoned (as usual) and riding my motorbike, a great combination. It must have been around 10.30 or 11 o'clock at night, and I decided I would ride to McDonald's. There was a branch a few miles away so, as I was starving, I thought I would go as fast as I could to get there.

There was a very long, sweeping bend in the road nearby. I always found it great fun to try and get my knee right down when I banked around that corner. I was riding as quickly as I could, loving the feeling of acceleration, enjoying the rush of tearing along on my bike and breaking the speed limit most of the way.

As I got near McDonald's, the long bend came into focus.

'OK,' I thought, 'lean into it. Get your knee down, keep the power on.'

So far so good.

My mistake was made when I lost my nerve.

With McDonald's in sight, I stormed around this corner. I had my knee just off the floor, I was really gunning it …

But then I felt as if I was going too fast and lost my bottle. I stupidly just touched the back brake pedal – and the next thing I knew, I was sliding across the floor in a mess of motorbike and headlights, ending up in a heap next to a lamppost.

I was lucky. If I had been a few inches out or been going a little bit faster, my head could have crashed into that lamppost. Fortunately for me, I hit the ground and slid into the kerb, smashing my elbow.

After lying there for a few self-pitying minutes, and having watched several people drive on past without stopping, I hauled myself upright. Somehow I managed to walk away with little more than some road rash on my legs, a few cuts and bruises and a sore elbow. Mostly it was my pride that was dented. There were some scuffs on the bike but they'd be easy enough to put right.

I made my way to McDonald's where, seeing me with blood down my jeans and a smashed up crash helmet in my hand, the guy on the counter asked, 'Are you OK?'

I must admit I was tempted to respond with something along the lines of, 'Can't you see I've just had an accident? Do I look OK to you, you idiot?' But somehow I refrained from that, mumbled something or other, asked if I could use the phone, and called home.

Nan answered. Sheepishly I told her what had happened, but that I was all right. She kindly offered to come and get me but, as the bike was still running, I decided to limp my way home by myself. When I eventually got back, a bit shaky and feeling slightly sorry for myself, Nan was waiting up for me. She gave me a hot drink and then ran me a bath. I climbed in and got myself cleaned up. I washed off the blood and the dirt, and eventually collapsed into bed, exhausted.

The next morning, I was feeling a bit bruised and sore, but after breakfast I set off to work as normal. The drugs deal was still on for that day, only I wasn't feeling right. My arm was hurting and starting to swell up, so I went to the site nurse and got it checked out. I was given some painkillers and sent home to rest. The nurse said there was a possibility that I had chipped my elbow. There wasn't much that could be done about it, but she told me to keep an eye on the swelling and, if it got any worse, to go to A & E.

That same lunch time, the 'big deal' went down. All my

buddies met up, drove to the dealer's house and bought the large-ish amount of dope. Then they went back to the training centre – where suddenly they kissed common sense goodbye and proceeded to smoke some of the gear in the back of the car … in the work car park. Someone happened to be walking by, got suspicious of all the smoke and noise bellowing out, and called the police. They all got arrested, and were carted off to the local police station.

The first I knew about it was when I got a phone call from one of the guys later in the day after they had been discharged from the nick.

Eventually they were dismissed from the college and gained a criminal record. I, on the other hand, was laid up at home with my arm throbbing, apparently having absolutely nothing to do with the deal and in the clear. A real close one!

So there I was, feeling as though I'd got out lucky, but the down side was that, on my return to work, I was under suspicion. The tutors all knew I was part of that group, only they could never actually pin anything on me. I wasn't there the day of the arrests; I hadn't given any money over, whereas my mates were all caught red-handed. On this occasion I was apparently innocent. However, the tutors made it more than clear that I was under close scrutiny. It felt like I couldn't even go to the toilet without being watched. To be honest, once all my friends had been fired and I was the only one left from that group, work started to get a bit tedious.

After a while, the time came when Laura, the girl on the south coast, and I were getting more serious. I was spending more and more of my time with her. Most weekends were taken up with going to see her and we were starting to do a lot of things together. Consequently, the girl I'd been seeing at home took a back seat. I've got to say, as unkind and selfish as it was, I pretty much just dropped her. She was great and we got on well; we were really good mates. But I was hooked on the older girl and eventually something had to give. I couldn't keep this up forever.

One long weekend, I went to visit Laura – and if my life seemed pretty out of control already, this was the point when it began to go completely pear-shaped.

My motorbike was due its MOT, and I needed to get back to Bristol after the bank holiday to get it done. I had just spent the weekend doing the usual things – getting high and drinking, doing a bit of socialising and having as much sex as I could possibly fit in. But the time was coming to make the journey back home. I wasn't looking forward to it; work was a bit boring now that it was so quiet. I didn't want to leave my girlfriend, but I knew I had to go.

The morning came and I got myself ready. I put my leathers on and was about to walk out of the house when I glanced through the window. To my utter disbelief, my bike was gone. I double-checked then hurtled down the stairs and outside. During the night, someone had taken a pair of bolt cutters to the security chain and stolen the bike. They must have broken the steering lock and simply cleared off. I couldn't believe it. I'd just got it looking great again. All the repairs had been done since my last spill and it was running really well. I was completely gutted.

I rang Nan to tell her what had happened and got in touch with the insurance people so that I could get the claim started. Then, as if nothing else mattered, I basically figured, 'Well, I'm stuck here now. I may as well stay …'

And that's what I did.

In one completely dumb moment, I kissed all reason and common sense goodbye. I jacked in my apprenticeship – I wasn't enjoying it any more anyway, so what the hell? – and decided I was going to stay in Bournemouth with Laura. I could figure out what to do from there.

Sadly, though, my figuring out didn't go so well.

In a few weeks, the insurance people got in touch. They said my motorbike was out of MOT so I wasn't going to get the full amount it was worth. I was really unhappy. Next to the drugs and my girlfriend, my bike was pretty much my only other love in life. I couldn't afford a new one, especially as I'd left my job, so I started to feel really sorry for myself. I began to get depressed. I felt as if I was stranded and, even though I could have gone home and at that point probably still have gone back to my job, I just wasn't thinking clearly.

So that was that. There I was, pretty much accidentally living on the south coast. OK, so I had no job, but at least I was with my girlfriend, right?

And that's when yet another monumentally stupid idea crossed my mind. When the insurance money for my bike came through, instead of putting it aside and saving it, why not spend it?

Basically, I just started getting wasted. Within no time at all, I'd pretty much blown the lot on drugs and drink.

Shortly after that, the summer holidays came round and Laura moved back home for the university break. I was left on my own, bored, with no job and no money, trying to figure out what on earth had happened and how I'd ended up in this position.

Someone suggested that I sign on the dole whilst I sorted myself out, but that was another mistake really. Once you're signing on it's very hard to get motivated again. I was getting my basic living expenses covered. I didn't need too much more and I just settled into a groove. I'm not sure I could have ended up in a worse situation if I'd planned it that way.

At least I managed to stay in a flat that belonged to a friend and, in my own lethargic way, tried to make the most of the summer. But all I was doing was getting high, bumming around, and waiting for my girlfriend to come back from her vacation. I'm not sure I even managed to get to the beach more than twice. I was flat and miserable and well on my way to developing a new art form: being a loser.

7

Manic Depression
(Jimi Hendrix)

THE SUMMER CAME AND WENT. I can't remember exactly what I did. I know I was signing on and getting stoned. And I watched Wimbledon. It was the year André Agassi came from nowhere and took the title. My girlfriend was travelling around Europe so I didn't see anything of her, just got the occasional postcard. My dad had moved to the south coast not long before, but I didn't see much of him either. I pretty much loafed all summer.

Eventually the new term started and when Laura returned, we moved into a house with a load of student friends. I was happy again. This girl had become the focus of my life and, to start with, things were going well. I was looking for work, we were involved in student-type stuff, partying and drinking, that kind of thing. I just wasn't doing any of the studying part.

As time went on, I was managing to get hold of drugs whenever I could, but I never did find any work I liked.

Eventually, I started getting miserable. My girlfriend was doing great at uni and I was slowly becoming a reclusive, depressed dead weight. It wasn't too long before tensions were beginning to show.

Late one night, one of our flat mates knocked on our bedroom door and asked to speak to Laura. She got out of bed and went to the lounge. I wasn't overly bothered and was probably stoned in any case, so I left her to it. She was gone for a while, and finally I summoned up enough interest to go and find out what was going on. To my surprise, I could hear all our friends in the front room of the house having a very hushed conversation, so I stood by the door and listened.

That was a bad idea.

'You've got to tell him.'

'When did it happen?'

'It's not fair on him.'

'What are you going to do now?'

My curiosity was now definitely piqued.

I opened the door to see my flat mates all sitting there, staring back at me with shocked faces. That's when I realised. They were all talking about us. About Laura and me.

I can't really remember what happened next, other than being given a brief explanation of what was going on, which is when I completely lost it. In short, Laura had been seeing someone else, our friends had confronted her over it, and this was the conversation I had just walked in on.

I was so hurt, not to mention angry and jealous. I just saw red. We started shouting and fighting and eventually she ran off to see this other guy, leaving me in a complete and utter mess.

I didn't know what to do. I felt as if the girl of my dreams had ripped the heart out of my chest and stamped on it till there was nothing left. I was devastated. All I wanted was to lash out – and I punched a hole through the front door of the flat.

I found out where this other guy was, too. He was staying in a student hostel only a few roads away, so I went round there and waited for him to answer the door. When he did, I snapped. I punched him as hard as I could right in the face. Instantly blood sprayed everywhere. I barged past him into his flat and confronted Laura. She was now in floods of tears and we screamed pointlessly at each other for a bit. Then eventually I left.

I was shaking and messed up. I really was completely alone … and my world had just fallen in on top of me.

I spent the next few hours wandering around Bournemouth late at night, before making my way home and trying to figure out what to do. I felt sorry for the guy I'd hit. In fact I felt terrible. I'd never hurt anyone like that before. Besides, when I stopped to think about it, he wasn't to know that Laura already had a boyfriend. So I made a point of trying to put things right with him.

In the meantime, Laura had decided she was going to move on. She had had enough of me.

Suddenly I had nowhere to go. I was so angry and hurt, and I felt as though the world was quite literally crushing me down.

I turned to more drugs and drink, whatever could take the pain away. I sank into depression and wished I was dead. Everything that mattered seemed to have been torn away. I even made a really poor attempt at suicide one night. If I'm honest, it was mainly a cry for help – but I half meant it.

It happened one night when I was feeling utterly depressed. Laura had gone home to her parents and I was alone. So I walked to the local off-licence, grabbed a cheap bottle of red wine, and drank it all. I then sat in the bathroom tentatively cutting my wrist. No one else was in the flat; they were all out.

The mess went everywhere. Blood has a habit of doing that, especially when mixed with a little water. The next thing I remembered was being on the sofa and practically passing out. Soon after, some of the guys came back to the flat and found me. They picked me up and washed me down. Then, when they realised that I wasn't going to die immediately and that the wounds were all superficial, they told me I had to go. I couldn't stay there any more, I was becoming a liability.

Another friend of mine shared a small flat just round the corner with his girlfriend. They'd been having some problems of their own so, as his girlfriend had decided to move out, my mate let me stay. I slept on the sofa. Before too long he moved back home to his family in the West Country, so I ended up staying in this tiny flat on my own. I met the owners, sorted out housing benefit and moved what little stuff I had in.

I hated it, though; I was lonely and still hurting desperately from the split with my ex. But I didn't feel as though I could go home to Bristol. I'd made such a mess of things. I even had a visit from my dad one day, but he kind of brushed off my break-up, just shrugging, 'You'll get over it. It happens to everyone.' Yet the pain in my heart was almost unbearable.

I started hanging out with a few guys who were dealing drugs. I didn't have any other friends. The guys from the previous flat didn't want to know me any more – I was too much of a burden for them – so these druggies soon became my closest mates. I also bumped into a local girl while I was in the nearby pizza shop, and soon I was seeing her, too.

I really liked her. She was into rock music like me, and horror books, and she also dabbled in the occult, tarot and astrology. Soon we decided she should move into my little flat instead of staying in her bed-sit.

I was doing more drugs now than before but at least I had a new girlfriend. I was also being hassled by the Job Centre to find work, which I didn't want to do. But eventually, with some encouragement from this new girlfriend, I took a position on a training scheme working with the Forestry Commission.

It was a three-month course designed to help people get their confidence back and encourage them back into the workplace. One thing was for sure: I definitely needed some confidence. Mine was down to zero. After everything that had gone on, self-inflicted or not, I was in a total mess.

Soon I was working in the forest, learning new skills and really enjoying myself. The trouble was that, as usual, my druggie radar kicked in. I met up with other guys on the course, and before long I was to be found as stoned as I could be without falling asleep in the forest or brush land surrounding the south coast!

The scheme ran its course and very quickly I was back to my old tricks.

My new girlfriend then encouraged me to find some more work, so I got a job in the bar of the BIC (The Bournemouth International Centre). Again, I actually really enjoyed it, and was soon pretty good at it, as well. However, my girlfriend also worked there part-time, and somehow we found ourselves too much in each other's pockets.

It wasn't too long before cracks appeared in that relationship, too. One day, after a season of yet more drugs, work and added stress, a friend who also worked at the bar started making trouble for us. Though I never really did get to the bottom of what had happened, I came home to find my stuff out on the stairs, and the door locked. I'd been kicked out. My girlfriend and I shouted at each other through the door but it got me nowhere – and my belongings were just lying in the corridor.

I was bewildered. Yet again, I plunged blindly into a tailspin. It was *my* flat; I had the tenancy agreement and the place was full of *my* things.

But instead of thinking it through, I just left everything where it was, and went to see my dealer.

8

Does Anybody Out There Even Care?

(Lenny Kravitz)

ONCE MORE, THERE I WAS FEELING SORRY FOR MYSELF, homeless, just been jilted and with no mates to speak of – and knocking on my dealer's door.

Despite what he did, he was actually a pretty good guy and had been through hell and back himself over the years. So he took pity on me and offered me a room in his flat. I grabbed the few possessions I had, which at the time included my very own cannabis plants, and moved in.

I went on to get stoned with a capital S and spent the next little while completely wasted, drowning my sorrows. I pretty much lost all concept of time around then. However, my new housemate was kind enough to sort out some food and, at least while I was staying there, I was fed well. I was still working at the Bournemouth International Centre so was able to give him some rent, but all the rest of my wages went on getting stoned.

My latest ex was still working at the Centre herself and, like me, was in a complete mess. I still don't really know what I was supposed to have done, but every time I saw her she would go mental. At times she would hit, kick and punch, or she would be a complete emotional heap. It wasn't long before I was pulled into the office and told, 'You've got to leave.'

I couldn't understand it. I hadn't done anything wrong. At least I was still turning up for work. But there was some major mud-flinging going on and the outcome was that I was for the chop. I took the bus back to my dealer's flat and simply told him, 'I've been fired and I don't know what to do.'

Things had gone from bad to worse. Up to then I'd had a bit of money coming in and could afford a few things. Now I was looking at no job and no hope. I was spiralling downwards pretty rapidly, hurtling my way towards another binge of drugs and booze.

Eventually, after I'm not sure how long, I went back to the dole. It took a little while and all the time I wasn't working I was using more and more drugs. I also started cashing cheques and ran up a pretty large overdraft; it was the only way I could get the cash I needed to buy drugs and food.

In the end, I moved from my dealer's spare room and found a flat in town to rent. I had my dole money and, on top of that, I started dealing to keep my habit afloat. I was trying desperately to keep myself from going completely off the rails, but anyone could see I was losing the battle.

The flat belonged to a friend who lived out of town. I let a mate stay on the sofa for a small fee. He was another druggie and was always up to some dodgy deal or other. We would spend our time getting wasted, doing a few deals and trying to meet girls, (he seemed a lot more successful than I was in that department). I was so deep into a pit by now that I'd even started messing with different cocktails of substances and booze. Christmas was looming, too, and that year it was nothing more than a blur. I do remember going out and getting loads of 'supplies', by which I mean yet more drugs and several bottles of booze. Then I simply bunkered up for the holidays. My mate went home to see his mum. My parents were in Derby. My dad was only an hour away but I didn't see him. I was miserable and lonely, and I pretty much smoked, snorted and boozed my way through that Christmas.

Hitting such a desperate point should really have been enough to snap me out of it all, but it wasn't. Things kept getting worse. I was still dealing – not massive amounts by any stretch and only to a few mates here and there, but enough to keep my own little habit going. The friend who'd been staying on my sofa would come and go, but by now the money he owed me for rent and food and stuff was mounting up. He must have figured he wasn't going to be able to pay me anything because he disappeared, never to be seen again, leaving me with more financial problems.

On top of that, my latest ex-girlfriend had found out where I was living and would occasionally call round at odd hours, usually after she'd been drinking. She'd be really aggressive, hitting me, swearing and cursing at me, then just leaving again. When I could, I'd pick up the occasional girl and bring her back to the flat. It was all a bit messy.

Around this time, I started scoring all my gear from new dealers. They only lived a few minutes' walk away, and were really screwed up. They were a couple – and both heroin addicts. Their flat was on the ground floor of a converted house, and whenever I went to get what drugs I needed, I would find myself fixated by all the paraphernalia of their seedy world – the darkness, the candles, the needles, the ligatures. I'd go round and score some gear, then I'd sit there and smoke a joint, and watch as they went through their routine. In the mess I was in, it was all starting to look very attractive. I could see the effects of the heroin on them. They looked so out of it; loving it.

No doubt about it, I was losing my grip on everything that was right. The world I had entered was dark, dingy and full of intrigue. And I was being sucked in. The more times I visited, the more appealing this couple's lifestyle was looking. I could feel the draw on my life. I started to ask them questions; to find out as much as I could – until I was just one step away from jumping into this black little hole with them …

One day, out of nowhere, I decided to give Nan a ring. I'd tried to keep in touch with her since I left, and even though I'd upset her by moving out and had made some stupid choices, I knew that I could always just call her. I don't remember all that I said. I probably told her a tale of woe and misfortune, laying the blame anywhere but with myself, but during the course of the conversation it came to light that my uncle had a flat sitting empty in Bristol.

By now I owed money to people all over the place for rent and drugs, and in a split second, I suddenly saw an opportunity to get out of Dodge. I contacted my uncle and we agreed that

I could move into his flat, for a reasonable rent. I jumped at the chance. I saw it as an opportunity to start afresh and get myself back on track. I knew I was heading for trouble if I stayed any longer where I was. I almost couldn't believe the timing.

I called Mum and Ian to tell them what was happening and somehow it got arranged that Ian would take the time off work, travel from Derby to Bournemouth, collect me and my stuff and help me get settled in my new flat. They knew very little of the actual mess I was in and I wasn't about to tell them, but I was extremely grateful for the help with moving.

Within a few days, I'd gathered all my bits together, packed whatever I needed, which really wasn't much, and was waiting for Ian to come and help me move.

Just at the moment we were about to drive away, my landlord arrived at the flat. I felt slightly cornered and made up some story about having to move quickly. I gave him my forwarding address with a promise of paying back what I owed him. Then, with the start of the engine, I was on my way out of Bournemouth for good.

For the first time in a couple of years of being in a completely hideous situation, it seemed as though there was finally some light on the horizon. I remember we listened to Lenny Kravitz in the car on the way back to Bristol. The sun was shining in my face and Ian and I laughed and joked. It was the first time in what felt like ages that I didn't feel totally alone.

When we arrived back in Bristol, it didn't take long to get moved into the new flat. And it was great – nice and clean, with two bedrooms, a lovely, large lounge and a bright pink bathroom (not that I cared about the colour!). It had a decent sized kitchen and overlooked the park, with its own balcony. I felt as if I'd finally come up smelling of roses. Ian ordered pizza, my older sister Sara joined us as she was still living in Bristol, and we celebrated the new start.

Shortly afterwards, Ian set off on the return journey back to Derby. What an awesome display of grace. He must have driven over 400 miles that day, just for me.

After Ian left, I'm guessing I must have unpacked, and then I vaguely remember hanging out with Sara for a while. We probably smoked several large joints. Looking back, this must have seemed like a very welcome moment of peace. I was in a new home and had escaped from a very bad nightmare … or so I thought.

What I didn't realise, and certainly wouldn't have been able to face up to at the time, was that I hadn't actually escaped from anything … because the nightmare began and ended with me.

I got myself back on benefits, half-heartedly looked for work, spent some time messing about on a newly-acquired guitar – and kept on getting stoned. After all, my old college buddies were only a phone call away. It was the easiest routine in the world for me to slip back into.

If we went out to someone else's house or to a party or club, we'd instantly meet up with other guys like us, and occasionally there'd be the opportunity to hit on some unsuspecting girl. It didn't take long before we'd all end up going back to my place to hang out. For days on end, my new home was full of druggies and the occasional girlfriend.

My existence was lived out in some kind of haze.

But there was something else now, too; something clawing at me. Inescapably.

I was finally beginning to realise what I'd become: I was an addict – and my addiction had me in an iron grip.

The worst of it was, I was powerless to do anything about it.

9

Heart Shaped Box
(Nirvana)

ON 5 APRIL 1994, the year I returned to Bristol, my hero, Kurt Cobain, killed himself. I was a massive Nirvana fan. I spent ages listening to their music and learning to play it on my guitar. I can remember clearly sitting on my chair, actually on my own for a change, watching the TV when the news came in that he'd committed suicide. He'd been in a drug-induced mess and shot himself.

I was so shocked. This guy and his music had been a huge influence on me, and suddenly he was dead. Gone, just like that. I made a couple of calls to friends and then reached for my usual comforter and got high.

During that time, I remember listening to Nirvana's *Heart Shaped Box*, and wishing with all my heart, 'If I could only be like Kurt Cobain.' And it was weird, but somewhere inside me, I seemed to hear a voice telling me that if I gave everything up, I would be rich and famous just like him … so I agreed.

I didn't know who I'd agreed with, although looking back, I guess it's pretty obvious. All I did know was that I wanted to be like Kurt … like my hero.

Amazingly, my guitar playing improved massively after that! I would spend all my time practising and working the music out. I finally had a focus, and when I did drugs, instead of watching TV, I'd play guitar. Many of the druggy mates I had were into music too so we'd get together and sometimes we'd just jam and get high.

And that's how the spring and summer passed.

It's funny, but even though I found myself in such a bad place, I really did want to be a force for good. I hated watching violent films and TV shows that were full of aggression. I honestly felt they were a bad influence and I'd rather watch something with a happy vibe to it. I would often sit around when people were over at the flat, spouting love and peace messages, though back then, my solution was through using drugs. On some level I seemed to figure that, at least if everyone was stoned or high, no one would want to hurt anyone; everyone could just love one another and get on.

One night when I was at home – it must have been heading into autumn by then because I remember it was dark – my flat mate, Sharon, was around and told me she had a friend coming over. He was a guy she knew from years back and, as she was training as a hairdresser at the time, she was going to cut his hair for him. I didn't think anything of it. I was used to people I didn't know coming round so I just carried on with what I was doing. I remember chilling out in my lounge when the doorbell rang.

Sharon went to answer it and came back in followed by this friend of hers called Pete. He seemed OK, nice enough, I thought, and they went into the kitchen to talk about what she was going to do. Pete had long, dark hair and wore silver earrings in both ears. In some ways he looked a lot like me, although there was something different about him, but I just couldn't put my finger on what it was.

We didn't really talk much, probably just made a few polite bits of conversation, but there was one thing that really stood out to me. I was rolling a joint on my lap and lit up, just as I had done thousands of times before, and I called to Pete, 'Do you want some?' Sharon rarely indulged so I didn't even bother to ask her. It was Pete's reply that caught my attention. He simply said, 'No, thanks.'

I was offended. I mean, who was this guy? He'd come into my flat and was probably the first person in possibly years who didn't want to do drugs with me; and I somehow knew I'd never be able to persuade him. These days I was feeling like some kind of peace and love guru – talk about deluded! I'd spend hours convincing myself and trying to convince others that the only way to make this world a better place would be if everyone got stoned. And yet here was Pete simply saying, 'No, thanks.' I remember feeling quite irritated as I shrugged, 'Well, that's your miss-out then.' And I slipped back into my own world. I don't know whether Pete noticed my annoyance. Sharon carried on cutting his hair and then he left.

He and Sharon were in touch again soon after that, and I know she saw him a few times. Then one night, she announced to me that she was going to church with him.

I've got to say I thought very little of it. I probably just sniggered quietly to myself about it.

Then came the night when Sharon got home buzzing. I'd never seen her so high, yet she wasn't stoned, or on anything else. I thought it was odd and asked a few questions about the church she'd been to. I wondered if she'd been brainwashed or something. To be honest, I was a little concerned and suspicious, but that soon passed. Getting high I forgot all about it, and it never really came up again.

Despite all my talk about peace and love, what was going on inside me was anything but peaceful. Have you ever had the feeling that someone is talking about you behind your back? I would often find myself filled with the sense that there were things going on around me that had a much deeper meaning than they appeared to have. All the drug abuse and the constant looking over my shoulder avoiding the law were starting to take their toll. I was becoming intensely paranoid. I was suspicious of everyone and deeply insecure, and what that did was turn me into more and more of a recluse.

I didn't know it at the time, but some of that 'feeling' was actually pointing at something very real happening to me. It turned out that Pete was a Christian, and he shared a flat with some friends of his in Bristol. Sharon, who realised what a desperate mess I was in and how much I needed help, had asked all of them if they would pray for me. So they did – and things started to get very weird, although as I say, I knew nothing of this at the time.

I was really struggling to keep it together. Among other things, I was getting very nervous around some of the people I knew, and rightly so. One of the guys I was getting my drugs from was involved in a little crime ring. I suppose these things often go hand in hand. One day, whilst doing my weekly visit to this dealer, I was given the strange invitation to go on a 'job'. Basically, I was being asked to go and do a robbery with this gang.

As I was so reclusive, fortunately the thought of going out to do anything was terrifying, so I made some excuse, kept my head down for a while and got out of it. It didn't end there, though. I was feeling more and more pressure to get involved with these people.

I was also beginning to hear and see things that weren't 'there'. For instance, I'd be chilling out and listening to some music, and the lyrics would literally jump out from the song as if someone was standing right next to me speaking the words. It was so strange. I was having visions, too, seeing pictures and having hallucinations which I thought was down to flashbacks caused by the acid and mushrooms I'd used. On top of that I was finding that, when I wasn't getting high, I was really starting to lose my cool. I was constantly twitchy and on edge. I was even having panic attacks. For no apparent reason, I'd find myself totally stressed and hyperventilating. I honestly thought I was starting to lose my mind. It was very scary. One time a friend of mine was over and he had to talk to me for about half an hour to try and convince me that I would be all right. I seriously thought I was going to die.

In the midst of this, I discovered that I needed to write. I turned out pages and pages of poetry and random thoughts that just seemed to flow out of me. Some were clear and helpful, others not so much. I would sit and write things down for literally hours on end. The words just kept pouring out. For days I would wake up, write, get stoned and then go back to bed. I knew things were all going very bad.

It was very rare for me to find any peace or quiet, or simply any personal space. There was often someone crashed out on the sofa or the floor and, because of my desperate need for company and the weak state of mind I was in, I just didn't have the capacity or the will to ask them to leave.

Something else, too. I knew that Sharon's boyfriend, one of my old drug buddies, had been treating her pretty badly. He was seeing other girls and sleeping with them behind her back. I was so torn. I wanted to tell her but I didn't know how. I was actually really fond of her – more than fond, really. On the other hand, her boyfriend was someone I'd been mates with for a long time.

After wrestling with it, I kept my loyalties to my mate and said nothing. Over the next few weeks, this left me with such raw feelings of shame and guilt that they started to consume me completely. Added to that I'd decided to tell Sharon of my real feelings for her, only to find that she didn't feel the same way. It was so weird for me. I was experiencing emotions I'd never felt before. Up until then, I hadn't really ever cared about much or about anyone except myself. This was something new and I felt as if I was being tormented. I literally wanted to curl up and die.

One particular day, I found myself lying on my bed praying, or maybe wishing, that I had a gun. Then I could just take my life away right there and then.

Once again, I think I was trying to make deals with unknown forces around me.

10

Where Is My Mind?
(The Pixies)

IT WAS VERY APPARENT that I was not in a good way. My mental health was in a bad state. Some days, if I had space in the flat, I would just sit in my chair, playing guitar all day without moving from the spot or even eating. Other days I would sleep the day away until someone came to visit, or I was crowded out in my own home by other druggies.

On other days still, I would sit in the kitchen staring out of the window over the park, trying to figure out what was going on and what was wrong with me. I was so messed up I didn't know which way to turn. I had no one I could trust or lean on. I was in a total mess.

From the kitchen window I had a great view. There was a long worktop right alongside it, and it was a perfect place to sit, smoke, think, and look out over the trees to the park beyond which was spacious and green. I would sit there for hours.

I was really confused as to why Sharon didn't respond to me, and I was feeling ashamed of my choices. I didn't like violence or aggression, and when I wasn't high, I hated that side of me. I wanted people to be kind to each other and to love one another – not treat each other like objects but as human beings with feelings, needs and emotions.

I started to come to the conclusion that I was different somehow. I didn't belong here. I didn't seem to fit the stereotypical male mould. I loved a lot, I cared a lot; I loved music and art and poetry. And I hated violence and cruelty, though most of those things seemed to be influenced by drugs.

One day I was chatting with one of my druggy mates and he was telling me stories of when he bullied kids at school. I remember I got so mad. When I was at school I was either on the receiving end of bullying or there were times when I was defending someone. I hated the values that surrounded me (or rather the lack of them). I hated the life I had. I knew that there was just something very different about me.

As I searched my soul, my thoughts and my emotions, the only idea that seemed to make any sense to me was that perhaps I was gay. To my messed up and confused mind it seemed logical. I was an emotional and caring person and I couldn't stand the violence that many of the people I knew liked, watched or got involved in. I knew even back then that the world was a messed up place and I just didn't fit into it. It may seem an odd conclusion, but with so much going on in my head, and without there having been anyone I could talk to or learn from for most of my life, it wasn't as great a leap as you might think. There was such a gaping hole in my heart, it was all I could come up with.

So that was it. Being gay, I'd decided, must be the answer. That was why I didn't fit in. That was why my heart was so easily broken. That was why I felt so different …

So now what?

It just so happened that my sister, Sara, called. She was going up to Derbyshire to visit my parents, so I figured I'd go along for the ride. I'd get some space, see Mum, have a good meal … and tell her, 'I think I'm gay.' Perhaps that would stop the torment I was in. Sara and I got sorted pretty quickly and left for the weekend.

I can't recall too much of the journey. I would have been stoned, for sure, though I do remember my sister still had her metallic blue Volkswagen beetle, which would blow cold air through the space where the stereo should be. This being the beginning of winter it wasn't a comfortable journey, and it took two and a half hours of driving before we arrived at Mum and Ian's.

It was good to be there, somewhere I could get some space. I expect we ate and laughed a bit. I remember sitting at the kitchen table chatting about loads of different things, putting the world to rights and generally blaming everyone and everything for the mess I was in. We sat up till quite late. I think Ian may have been away that weekend, or busy somewhere, as I don't remember seeing him around. But then so many of the details are hazy, as I was high as usual. It was only the punctuating moments that seemed to stick.

I don't know how long we sat there chatting, but after a good while it was time to crash out. It was getting late and was pitch black outside so, sitting with Mum at the kitchen table, I rolled a large joint, said goodnight and went into the garden to smoke it. I decided I'd have a private chat with her in the morning and tell her everything.

When I came in from the cold, I closed the back door, climbed the stairs and settled into bed in Mum's spare room. It was actually the study. There was a whole wall of books down one side – all kinds of books, fact and fiction, novels and biographies, and it was always a bit untidy. Mum's teaching stuff was piled everywhere. There were baskets overflowing with creative material and papers, and there I was, lying on a mattress on the floor in the middle of it all.

I decided to put the radio on to listen to some music whilst I drifted off to sleep. I messed with the tuner and eventually found Radio One, then lay there trying to drop off.

My mind was still spinning with all the stuff that had been going on recently – and with 'the conversation' I was going to have with Mum the next day. I was overcome with such a feeling of desperation that it was almost completely crushing me. The thought of telling my mum what was happening and the conclusions I'd come to about my sexuality was unsettling. As a family we never talked much, and certainly not about feelings, emotions and thoughts. There has always seemed to be a closed-ness about those topics. We could spend hours debating, moaning, criticising and analysing, but the reality of exposing my deepest thoughts and emotions would be no easy task.

Eventually I started to drift off. Pictures and images began floating through my mind.

I was entering into that half-awake, half-dreaming phase, with the radio playing in the background, when suddenly, out of nowhere, a voice spoke to me. It was similar to the time I was listening to music back at the flat. Only, this time it made me jump; this time it sent chills through me.

My heart must have skipped a beat. It felt as though someone was literally right behind me. The voice sounded deep and terrifying – as were the words I heard spoken:

'Turn around.'

I froze where I lay. I don't think I could have turned around even if I'd tried. A feeling of fear gripped me completely.

What if there was someone there? Who was it? Was it God speaking? Was it the devil? After all, I'd wished that I would die. Perhaps the devil had come to take me. I'd dabbled a little in the occult with a previous girlfriend so had some awareness of spirituality, and was clearly experiencing things here that were not of this world.

Terrified and frozen with uncertainty, I did what all grown men do when they are scared at night in the dark in a strange room … I pulled the duvet over my head, curled up and prayed, 'Help me, God. Keep me safe …' Something along those lines anyway, and finally I drifted off to sleep.

The next morning when I woke, the radio was still playing quietly and the sun was shining through the curtains.

I felt strangely peaceful and looked round to find there was no one in the room but me. I'd had a good night's sleep. I felt rested. Better.

Eventually, I went downstairs to the kitchen and had breakfast. I can't say I remember much of the rest of the day very clearly at all. However, I did feel so much more relaxed that in the end 'the conversation' with Mum never happened. Somehow I didn't feel I needed to have it. Everything seemed fine. When I'd woken that morning, the torment I'd been feeling had left me, and there was no need to say anything. Things just seemed different.

That night, Sara and I drove back home to Bristol. I've never questioned or struggled with my sexuality again.

11

Speakeasy
(Shed Seven)

AFTER COMING HOME FROM DERBY TO BRISTOL, I lost all concept of time. I don't know how long it was between that weekend and the next set of events that occurred; it could have been days or weeks. Nothing else was really any different. I was still into the same things, the same routine, and I still had the same issues, yet they just didn't seem to be affecting me with quite the same intensity.

However, that was about to change.

It was the weekend before Christmas of 1994. I'd been invited to a party. It was a friend's birthday in town somewhere, and a few of us had been asked to go along. I've never been much of a party kind of guy. I guess the feeling of being around people that I didn't know scared me, and I was still as reclusive as ever. In the end, after a bit of coercion, I agreed to go. At least I felt I could cope if I was booze and substance fuelled.

Sharon was driving. As always, she was the only one of my friends who did. In fact, she was the only one with a job and a relatively level head. We piled into the car and set off. Once again, I couldn't tell you where the party was, how long it took to get there, or anything about it, really. I just remember a smallish room, with a bar and tables, and walking in feeling anxious and self-conscious.

I walked up to the bar to order some drinks and, to my surprise, right next to me was Pete, Sharon's Christian friend. For some reason I was really pleased to see him there. I said hello, got my drink and then went to sit down. Pete stayed by the bar.

As the evening went on, I found myself so much wanting to chat to this guy who I'd only met once before. I didn't know much about him, except by now that he was into church. Though I wasn't interested in all that, I had a good feeling about him and I thought I'd at least be able to talk to him. So over I went. I ordered a drink and we got into conversation.

Music was playing loudly as we started chatting … and the next thing I knew it was time to go home. It was incredible! We'd just talked and talked.

I poured out my heart to him. I told this stranger all that had been going on – with the flat, my life, my heartache, my ideas about violence and hate, every thought in my head; even my feelings on drugs making the world a kinder, more chilled place. I explained my theory that if everyone was high, they wouldn't be worried about all the other rubbish. I told him everything and Pete just listened.

I don't know how long he sat there with me. He didn't seem to say very much at all, though I clearly remember he told me something about false prophets giving messages that lead people away from the truth. I felt as if he was talking about me and my theories, and I knew I didn't want to be a person like that. He also mentioned God, church and Jesus.

Finally, just as I was about to leave the party, he invited me to a church meeting the next day.

'Hah!' I thought. 'Me? Go to a church meeting? A carol service of all things!'

It's clearly the last place on earth I would consider going. The last time I was in church I was about 13 years old and in the scouts, and I spent the whole time messing around. It was dreary and tedious and there really was no life there. Why would I want to go to church?

On the other hand, I didn't consider that I'd even be welcomed in church. I was smelly and unkempt. My hair was long and matted, and I had piercings in my ears and nose. People would cross the road rather than be anywhere near me, let alone want me around. I was used to getting odd looks, especially from the other flat owners in the block I lived in. I think they were terrified of me. I did look quite a sight. Pete reassured me that I would be all right and he seemed genuine enough. Sharon even said she'd go too, so reluctantly I agreed. 'Ok, ok, I'll go. See you tomorrow.'

So we left the party. I don't know what happened to everyone else. They must have gone their separate ways. Sharon dropped me back home, and I arranged to get a lift with her to church the next evening.

My head was spinning with all the thoughts and conversations I'd just had. Was I a false prophet? Was this stuff Pete had been telling me true? What about God? Jesus? Truth? Lies? Deception?

Questions, questions … Anyhow, I'd agreed that I'd go to this meeting, and I've always tried to be a man of my word so, with that, I concluded I'd be there. What's the worst that could happen, huh?

I settled into bed and then I crashed out.

It never dawned on me that the next day would be one I'd never forget.

I woke up when the phone rang. It was a mate of mine. He wanted to score some gear and I didn't have any in the flat except for myself, so we arranged to meet up later to go and get some from a dealer I knew in town. It was only a few miles away and I sat at home and waited for him to arrive.

I was very aware that I'd made a promise to go to the church meeting later that day and was anxious to be back home in time to meet Sharon for my lift. It was really odd. I very rarely left my home, let alone to go somewhere as unusual as church. Still, I'd agreed to go and I didn't want to let Pete down. I felt strangely compelled to make sure I went to that meeting.

When Steve, my mate, eventually arrived, he came with a friend of his who I didn't know. That put me on edge immediately. He looked rough and nearly as messed up as I was. He was clearly a druggy himself, and ordinarily if I'd met him I'd have been cool about it, but today for some reason I was nervous.

Druggy circles are full of suspicion and paranoia. You never know who is watching or listening to what you're up to, and there are certain unspoken rules that you stick to – a bit like the pirates' code in Johnny Depp's *Pirates Of The Caribbean.*

Introducing mates unannounced when you're about to go to your dealer definitely went against the rules. This guy could have been anyone. He might have been the fuzz at worst, or just plain indiscreet at best. How was I to know? I'd made a promise to be somewhere and the last thing I wanted was to get busted today.

As if that wasn't enough, we went down to the car park and got into a car with a smashed back window. No one said anything, but I got the distinct impression it was stolen. Tension was rising as we set out on a mission to score.

I remember sitting in the back of that car, being driven through some of the roughest parts of Bristol. It was a clear, cold day and I was not happy, feeling extremely conspicuous in this motor, not to mention being freezing. I was half expecting to be pulled over and nicked at any moment. But despite being so on edge about the whole situation, for some reason I just went along with it, yet again allowing my circumstances to dictate the outcome of my life.

Amazingly, we got to the dealer's house unnoticed and, fortunately for me, I was in and out without a hitch. Yet somehow I couldn't shake the distinct feeling that the whole day was starting badly. Even though on the surface it wasn't much out of the ordinary for the kind of lifestyle I was leading, I felt that I was being distracted from the promise I had made to go to the church meeting that evening. Somehow, everything I was doing seemed to have massive significance – as if there was some kind of unseen tug of war going on.

We made our way to Steve's place. I was expecting his mate just to drop him off and then run me home, but his mate wasn't interested in taking me back to my flat. He was only after some gear of his own, and as soon as he'd got what he wanted, he left us at Steve's and cleared off.

So, there I was, several miles from home – and even if I could have figured out the way back to the flat, I was so agoraphobic that to walk that far was near impossible for me. I was stranded and extremely concerned. We didn't have mobile phones back then, and I wasn't sure I'd be able to get hold of Sharon, let alone be at the flat for my lift. I don't think I had any money for a bus either.

My anxiety levels were going through the roof, so, true to the druggy spirit in times of stress … I got wasted.

I was trying to keep an eye on the time and by now I had made a few calls to try and track Sharon down. But at the same time, Steve and I were getting high and phasing in and out of reality. Even though I'd left messages at the flat and with a few mates in the hope Sharon would get back to me at Steve's, I wasn't sure what to do. I was getting panicked and time was flying. It was already getting dark outside, and all I felt was useless and tense.

Eventually Sharon did ring. She'd been back to the flat to get me and had picked up the message I'd left for her. She agreed to come and find me at Steve's and take me to the meeting as planned. I felt a disproportionate sense of relief flood over me.

Things were going to be all right. I could keep my promise.

My emotions were all over the place. Anxiety and the effect of all the drugs, combined with my deep desire to fulfil a promise, made it feel as though there was a very real battle raging within me. I felt I was being tugged and pulled from every direction. On the surface it was just a slightly unusual day, but underneath I was beginning to sense much greater forces at work in my life.

It wouldn't be long before I realised just what was at stake.

12

Changes
(David Bowie)

WHEN SHARON ARRIVED, I SAID GOODBYE to Steve and we quickly got on our way to the carol service. There were three of us in the car and we headed for the Pentecostal church at the bottom of Ashley Road in Bristol. It was dark and slightly chilly, and you could see your breath in the air.

There was a warm glow from the streetlights as we pulled up right next to the church. It's a pretty looking building, with a high tower, right on the edge of the road. We got out of the car and made our way over to the door.

I was stoned and a bit nervous. Going anywhere new would get me anxious let alone to a church meeting, but I'd agreed to come, so here I was. I was wearing dirty, torn and probably smelly clothes; my hair was long and greasy and messy. I had multiple piercings in my ears and nose and I hadn't shaved for ages. I looked rough. This was the first time since childhood I'd been inside a church building and it felt really alien. I took a deep breath and stepped through the door.

The meeting had already started. Pete was there to greet us and we made our way to the seats.

To be honest, I don't remember too much of the meeting. There were no flashing lights or blinding revelations. There were some carols and some kind of talk, and there were some seemingly crazy people shouting out what I took to be prayers or something like that. I just sat there taking it all in – probably with my mouth wide open.

However, I had a real sense of feeling welcome, and somehow I just felt warm throughout. There was something different about these people. I sat through the service, trying to pay attention, but I can't say I can recall anything that was said. It was all right, though – not as scary as perhaps I was expecting – and then it was over.

We left the main part of the building and went out to the annex where we were greeted by loads of people. They all seemed really pleased to see me. I was not at all used to that kind of welcome. Normally people would close the door or give me strange looks. This was unsettling.

Very quickly I started to get fidgety. I'd been in the meeting for about an hour and obviously hadn't smoked anything for the whole time, and you can imagine that the buzz of earlier was wearing a little thin. So I made my excuses and went outside. Someone came with me. We lit cigarettes and got into a conversation, probably about going home or something else really mundane, but then the weirdest thing happened.

I distinctly remember saying, 'I could really use a cup of tea right now,' when, as if on cue, a tall, blond guy I'd never met before came outside with a cup and saucer. He handed it to me with a huge grin on his face and said, 'I thought you might like a cup of tea.'

I was flabbergasted! That was really freaky. I wasn't used to being around people who were this kind and friendly. On top of that, I felt like this guy must have read my mind. I was sincerely taken aback, not only by the surreal timing but also by this really simple gesture of kindness.

I drank my tea, finished my cigarette and then we went back inside where I was properly introduced to this tall guy – yet another Pete. We chatted for a while and then he and all his friends, including the other Pete, were leaving the meeting to go back to his house for a coffee and chill. They invited me to join them. I didn't have anywhere else to go and they all seemed friendly enough, so I did.

Myself, Sharon and her friend, along with the two Petes and the rest of *their* friends, walked up the road to what was affectionately known as 'the boys' flat'.

The flat was just a few minutes away, and we settled in the lounge with a cuppa. It was a simple place, tidy and clean – nothing unusual there but it was strange being surrounded by all these Christians. I'd never met people like this before. They all seemed larger than life somehow. I couldn't tell if it was simply confidence or the fact that a couple of the guys were just plain tall, and I'm only five foot nine!

Whatever it was, there was something about them that was completely different from anyone else I'd ever met before.

I was sitting on the sofa, chatting away in the lounge, when I was suddenly acutely aware that my language was really, really awful. I knew I swore a lot (everyone I knew did the same), but in these guys' company, I realised just how bad it was. It's not that they said anything or pointed it out; they were far too gracious. I just became so aware of it, maybe because they didn't use bad language at all. Every other word I spoke was f*** this and f*** that. It was as if each time I opened my mouth, it sounded as though some clanging bell was ringing, and the words fell to the ground with a thud. I felt really self-conscious.

There was one guy there called John. He was a smoker and at one point we both sat out on the porch, rolling cigarettes and chatting. He seemed nice enough and we connected. I remember telling him some of the things happening in my life and he was very understanding. We laughed a lot sitting there, too.

The evening drew on, and eventually Sharon and her other friend wanted to go home. Sharon had to work the next day. As we were discussing leaving, one of the guys from the flat happened to mention there was a spare bed if I wanted to stay the night. That way I could chat more if I felt like it, rather than disappearing off in a hurry. I gave it some thought and decided to stay. I knew full well there were going to be people crashed out at mine that evening; it was often the way. My best mate and some of his friends would go and hang out there because it was easier for them to do drugs at my place rather than in their own homes. Most of them were still living with their parents, so my flat was an easy place to find drugs and get wasted. I never seemed strong-willed enough to tell them not to. So, with the offer of a break, I thought I'd take the chance to chill out and make the most of the respite from my miserable little life, even if it was just for a night. I felt safe and welcome, and I figured it would do me good.

So Sharon left and I made myself comfortable, chatting, getting to know a few of the guys there.

As was usual for me, I lost pretty much all concept of time. Finally, the rest of the guys either went home or went to bed, and I went to the spare room, which I was sharing with another guy, called Olli.

We chatted for ages. You'd have thought we'd known each other for years as we sat cross-legged on the bed. It was almost like kids at a sleepover.

I poured my heart out about all the drugs, the lifestyle, the effect it was having on me, the broken relationships – absolutely everything. We must have talked till the early hours of the morning. Other than the night I'd spoken to Pete at the party, I'd never been that honest with anyone. It felt liberating.

When we eventually settled down to sleep, I fell into a very deep and peaceful rest.

The next morning I woke around 6.00am. There was some movement out in the hallway. Some of the guys were up already.

But even though it was early, I was refreshed. Not only that, I'd been having the most amazing dream. Before that night, I would have conversations with people at my flat about dreams, but I never dreamt myself. Ever. My friends did, and they'd often tell me about them. I even had a dream dictionary and would give them some ideas about what they might mean. But I never actually dreamed myself.

I was stunned, not only because of my dream, but because I could remember it so clearly. More than that, I was dreaming about heaven … And I was there.

I could picture it all: there were vivid features, towers, translucent walls, beautiful architecture, amazing colours and moving lights. And such a feeling of peace rested on me, I was almost overwhelmed. What was going on?

When I got up to join the others for breakfast, I immediately felt different somehow. I couldn't explain it, but *everything* felt different. Miraculously, I found that I didn't want to do drugs! I didn't even want to smoke a cigarette! I had absolutely no cravings at all, nothing. It was incredibly odd and overwhelming. I mean, what was happening to me? This was not normal. I'd never felt anything like it before.

Usually the first thing I would do when I woke was smoke a cigarette. Then I'd reach for my stash and get wrecked. I'd been doing that for years. Whatever I had handy I'd take it: speed, grass, dope. That was how I coped with life. This was my existence; my routine. It was how I managed; how I got by.

But not this morning.

Somehow there was no desire, no aches, no shakes; just peace.

What on earth was happening?

I stepped out of the spare room and John walked by.

He asked me for a light and said I was welcome to join him for a smoke, to which I responded, 'No thanks.'

I passed him my Zippo – 'Oh, by the way, you can keep that. I don't need it any more.'

Huh??

What had I just done? Every smoker loves his Zippo! It's like an extension of himself. I was very proud of mine. Nan had bought it for my 16th birthday – and I'd just given it away! John was as surprised as I was. He even double-checked with me.

'Keep it,' I replied. 'I don't need it now.'

Now that was weird. What was this? Had I suddenly grown some self-control? It was as if someone else was speaking for me, but at the same time, this *was* me.

The guys in the flat were meeting for an early morning Bible study and prayer time, and they kindly invited me to join them. I went along and sat in on this really odd little gathering. I'd never been to a Bible study or prayer group before. They were talking about this little black book, together with a lot of other things that just went over my head, but they seemed so interested in it all. So I listened to what was said. Then they chatted and after that, they prayed. They *all prayed*. Out loud! As if there was someone actually listening ...?

I felt odd. I didn't know if I ought to be saying something, but I had no idea what or who to say it to. So I sat silently, letting it all go on around me. What was this strange little group I'd found myself in the middle of? It felt so peaceful.

Eventually everyone set off to work. All except one. He was a foreign guy called Harjit, an ex-Muslim from Malaysia, and he was studying at a local college to become a vicar or something. He was going to be around for the day so was happy for me to hang out with him. As there was no pressure for me to leave, we went to the kitchen and started talking. I was in a bit of a spin so having someone to chat to was really helpful. I needed to try and understand what was going on, and here was someone who was happy to talk me through it.

13

Jesus Is Just Alright
(Doobie Brothers)

WE SAT IN THE KITCHEN ALL MORNING, drinking coffee and hot chocolate, and eating. We wandered to the shops and bought some groceries. I was still having absolutely no cravings or shakes. Nothing. It was so odd. How could this be happening? Whatever it was, it kept me asking questions all day.

Harjit told me all about his life, his family back home, and how he'd left Malaysia to study in the UK. He kept mentioning Jesus, and that he'd met Him, and he kept telling me that Jesus could sort me out; Jesus could help me get my life right.

Jesus could get me off drugs.

I didn't fully grasp what he was saying, I just figured I'd listen and ask questions. I was really enjoying the company.

There was something else, too; something resonating deep within me.

Later that day, a few more guys came to visit and I was introduced to them, as well. One of them was doing a YWAM (Youth With A Mission) course, whatever that was, and he also began telling me all about Jesus.

There were a few more visitors throughout the day, and it was the same with all of them. They kept talking about Jesus. All day long. I mean, who was this Jesus?

The time drifted on and, as I didn't need to be anywhere, I wasn't bothered at all. Evening came round, and the rest of the guys got back from work or college. Pete, I think, was working at a bike shop in town. Dan was doing a few odd jobs. Nick might have been studying.

Harjit had prepared some food during the afternoon, and we all ate together. I really felt at home here. Everyone was so genuine, not like the druggies I was used to spending time with who only wanted to be around you so they could get high. These guys welcomed me in. They showed grace, kindness and generosity like I'd never known.

As the evening went on, the doorbell started ringing and even more people began arriving at the flat, some with guitars, others with their Bibles. They were all so friendly, part of a group of young people from different local churches who met to pray and worship most Monday evenings, and tonight was no exception.

At least, it was no exception for them. For me, however, this was to be the single most significant night of my entire life.

As people arrived, we gathered in the lounge. I was introduced to a few other guys – Jon and Noel who played guitar – and there were lots of girls too; Wendy, Sarah, Mel. I can't remember how many people there were altogether. Then some older folks arrived to keep a watchful eye on things.

Eventually, 'Big Pete' asked if I'd like to be prayed for, and I figured … why not?

So, as I sat on the sofa, a few of the guys gathered round me, put their hands on my shoulders and started to pray. All the time there seemed to be more people coming into the flat, playing their guitars, singing and worshipping this Jesus that they wouldn't stop talking about.

I didn't know what to expect or what to do. I'd never been prayed for before. All I could do was close my eyes.

Almost immediately, I started to feel a tingling sensation in my fingers. It was like pins and needles but not at all painful. This sensation set my mind racing. What were they doing to me? Was this some psychic thing going on? What was happening?

I'd never experienced anything like it before, even with all the drugs I'd been doing and the hallucinations I'd had. The tingling spread to my hands and they were starting to get hot. I felt as if I was catching fire.

That was when Harjit spoke to me: 'Jason, if you want to know the Lord Jesus, just tell Him.'

I was feeling hot and the tingling all over my hands started to spread up my forearms. My head was spinning, but I was beginning to come to the conclusion that, if Jesus was as real as they said He was, if He could do what they said He could, and if this sensation was normal and something to do with God … then I must be in safe hands.

I mustered up all the strength I could find within me and said the first prayer I had ever prayed out loud to Jesus.

It began like this – 'Jesuuu …'

And then, *bam*!

At that moment I was completely consumed from head to foot by the sensation that was sweeping through me. I felt like a ball of fire – and I fell to the floor.

I can't tell you how long I lay like that, or much about what was going on around me. I guess the rest of the people were worshipping and praying. I remember being curled up in the foetal position, unable to move. I felt as though I'd stuck my finger in a power socket and had been shocked into some kind of muscle spasm. Every last inch of me was burning. I had never, ever experienced anything like this.

I began to toss and turn. I think I was probably being delivered of some demons. Then, after some more time of this incredible power surging through me, I ended up lying on my front and I remember reaching out and grabbing hold of someone's feet. It was as if I needed an anchor point. I had been thrown around all over the floor for what must have been quite some time, and I was exhausted.

Finally, I started to come round and feel more normal. I was still on fire, though with less intensity, and I was trembling all over. I managed to sit up. The people around me seemed happy and excited. All I wanted was to know what on earth had just happened to me.

I think someone must have explained to me that I had been

touched by the Holy Spirit, and that He had healed and delivered me, or something like that. I can't recall in any detail exactly what was said. It wasn't till later that I began to comprehend fully what had gone on.

All I knew at that precise moment was that I had just met God.

Later I was to learn that I'd been 'born again'.

I sat there on the floor, unable to say much. I couldn't even begin to express myself. I didn't know whether to laugh or cry. When the emotion of the experience finally overwhelmed me, I sobbed and sobbed and sobbed. Harjit held on to me as I wept. He assured me that it was all right. I'd just met Jesus, I'd been filled with the Holy Spirit, and Jesus loved me and would never let me go. I felt like jelly, huddled there, crying uncontrollably.

Later that evening when some of the emotion had subsided and almost everyone had gone home, I went back to the spare room where I was to stay another night. I was reflecting on all that had been happening and pouring out my heart to God, telling Him everything, and somehow being able to forgive all the people who had ever hurt me in the past. I just couldn't help it. It was flowing out of me unstoppably.

As I prayed, I could remember that I'd heard the guys in the lounge praying in a strange language, and I wondered if I could do that, too. I opened my mouth and immediately discovered I could! A whole new world was opening up to me; I was now doing what I later understood to be 'speaking in tongues' – praying to God in a special language that He had given to me.

I've never touched drugs again since that day. For that matter, I've never been tempted to either. I've never even experienced any withdrawal symptoms.

So, here's the deal. From early on I was hooked. I'm an all or nothing kinda guy.

For years I'd been abusing drugs and my body. It really was my entire life. That was what I did. When I wasn't high I was thinking about getting high. When I was high I was thinking about getting higher. If I wasn't high I was depressed. If I was running low on gear I'd be thinking about getting more. That was it. My mates were the same. My life revolved around drugs. Everything revolved around drugs. Addiction was just part of the deal.

When you understand that, to say that I was suddenly free from all the effects of drugs and addiction is no small matter. If you know anyone with an addiction, or have one yourself – booze, porn, food, smoking, gambling, shopping, drugs – have you noticed how it just doesn't go away? It's not something you can simply stop on your own. That's why it's an addiction – and, believe me, I know. Even early on, before the drugs had got a real hold on me, I'd wanted to give up smoking, but no matter how hard I tried, I just couldn't do it. I'd maybe last a few hours if I was lucky, but the hold was too strong.

Addiction is an illness. It's a truly desperate problem … And there I was completely free from it. Overnight! No shakes, no sweats, no pangs, nothing … That's not just an incredible story. The freedom I received was nothing short of a miracle.

Another thing that always fascinates me about the way I met

Jesus was that it didn't happen the way you're generally given to understand – you know, the whole 'believe, repent, receive' thing; the way books tell you or the way you're taught through training. God touched me, healed me and loved me way before I knew anything about Him; way before I ever did any training; way before I really knew who Jesus was or what the Bible said.

It makes me smile how we all have our small, human concepts of how God does what He does. But then something miraculous happens, and it reminds us that God is God – and He'll do what He likes, when He likes, how He likes. All our plans and programmes and clever strategies are nothing compared to learning to walk closely with God and listening to what He has to say to us. After all, when you look at Jesus in the Gospels, He rarely did anything that was expected of Him. Things just happened because He was there walking in tune with the Father.

There's no doubt it's a risky business, but maybe we still need to learn to let God be God …

14

Brand New Day
(Sting)

TUESDAY MORNING CAME ... the morning following my encounter with God.

I woke up as a brand new person. I was still in a bit of a daze but I felt different – whole, healthy and strong. I was pretty thin as all the drugs had taken their toll on my body – I was only about nine and a half stone – but I was determined to get my life straight. Suddenly I had a sense of purpose and a reason to care. I decided I would cut out all addictive substances from my lifestyle. I stopped drinking tea, coffee and beer – and never experienced even the slightest headache.

I borrowed a bike from one of the other guys and cycled several miles to my flat, which was unheard of for me. I felt as if I had a fiery hand in the centre of my back, pushing me all the way. When I arrived, I let myself in and found a few of the druggies still there, crashed out on the sofa and around the place.

I didn't hesitate. I told them I'd found Jesus and no longer wanted to have anything to do with that drug-fuelled lifestyle. I asked them point blank to leave, even though some of them were friends of Sharon's, who was still living in the spare room, and another of my best mates, Matt, was there, too.

But I'd made my point and that was that. It was *my* flat and things were going to change.

Admittedly there were a few noses put out of joint – even Sharon was a little offended – but I didn't care. It had to stop, and I was no longer going to have this stuff going on in my home. I've got to say they were all a bit taken aback, and made some pretty negative comments, but it didn't bother me. I wanted a clean slate. I needed a fresh start. So I insisted, and eventually they all left.

I had my flat back and a new life to lead.

Next I went through all my belongings. I cleaned out all the occult and new age stuff, the dreams stuff, all my druggie paraphernalia, all the porn, everything I had that was to do with dealing – absolutely everything. If it had something to do with my old life, it had to go. I pulled back the curtains, opened the windows, took down the Kurt Cobain posters, cleaned the flat from top to bottom, and pulled all my music down off the shelves and stored it in a pile. Later, rather than dump it all, I decided to sell the records. I didn't have any money and I figured they'd be worth a few quid.

Then I ran a hot bath and jumped in. I took out all my piercings – the earrings, nose rings, nipple piercing. And I had a shave – for the first time in years! I was a new man and

I was going to show it. I felt as if I'd been given my life back and I wanted to make the most of it. Starting right now.

The rest of the week was simply amazing. Things were changing in me and around me at a staggering rate.

After cleaning up the flat, I went back to the guys' house to hang out with them. I was eager to know what was happening to me and there was no shortage of people around to encourage and show me things that the Bible said. I was also given a Bible of my own. I still have it and read it regularly to this day, though it's getting a bit tired and battered now.

I came to understand that what I had experienced that Monday evening was the baptism of the Holy Spirit that is spoken about in the book of Acts, and that I'd been 'born again', just the way Jesus spoke of to Nicodemus in the Gospels.

One day at the boys' flat, I was sitting in the lounge on my own, and found I had the most incredible strength in my body. I was no fitness fanatic, and I certainly wasn't very healthy after all the drug use, but I discovered that I could push myself up into a full handstand from sitting on the floor! Even my body felt new. This was amazing.

It was an incredible feeling to know I had just encountered the living God and that He loved me. I was desperate to tell people what had happened. I made phone call after phone call. I just couldn't contain this good news. I rang my family, who were shocked and not just a little concerned. I rang old friends, everyone I could think of. I was met with a mixture of different responses, but I couldn't stop myself wanting to talk about it.

On the evening of Wednesday 21st December, a large group of us went out for dinner at a Mexican restaurant in town. I was so full of energy, I was ready to talk to anyone, and had many opportunities to share what God had just done for me. It was so exciting. I was loving having such a great story to tell.

During that meal, I found myself playing with the necklace I was still wearing. It was something I'd worn for some time and was actually one of my prized possessions. I had got it for a few quid at a new age festival a while before. It was the Hindu symbol Om or Aum, and was about the size of an old English penny and made of silver.

As I held it, it felt strangely dirty to me somehow. Then, suddenly, it just came away in my hand. It was as if the knot holding it round my neck was simply untied for me.

At that moment, what seemed like a great weight lifted off my shoulders, and I dropped it on the table as if it was red hot. I realised it was yet another thing that had to go. I don't know how, but I'd missed it earlier.

As I left the restaurant that evening, I threw it away, and I heard the Holy Spirit whisper to me, 'Silver for gold.'

I felt a great sense of peace flood over me that night, and I quickly learned that what I was to leave behind for God would be replaced with something of much greater value.

Immediately after throwing the necklace away, I found a pound coin on the floor, and I walked home smiling to myself.

I soon started to discover that God was eager to talk to me, as He is to anyone who will listen to Him. I could hear the Holy

Spirit speaking in my heart, and I found I knew things ahead of time. For example, if the doorbell rang, I knew who it was. Or I seemed to know when the phone was about to ring. I even knew where to find things in cupboards I'd never looked in! I was amazed. It seems very obvious to me now, but all the time the Holy Spirit was teaching me to know His voice.

I was so excited that God, the Creator of the universe, wanted to talk to me. I was gutted that I'd somehow missed out on this all my life and no one had told me about it before. And I was desperate to develop this relationship. I felt so special, it was overwhelming. I would pray in tongues for hours, laughing, crying, and enjoying my new friendship.

One day of that first week with God, I remember walking to the front door, having just been to the shops. I was searching through the bunch of keys I was holding for the one to the flat, and at the same time asking God, 'Why me? Why have You done this for me? I don't deserve it. After all, I was pushing drugs, doing drugs, treating people so badly and living a totally selfish life.'

At that moment, as I picked the last key on the bunch, God spoke. Whether it was in my heart or externally I couldn't tell you, but I heard Him speak so clearly it was as if He was standing right beside me: 'Because you are the last one you'd expect.'

And that was right. No one would have expected me to find God. No one. It was as big a shock to everyone else as it was to me.

The next morning, I found myself with a huge desire to cut my hair and get myself cleaned up even more. All the rest of the guys had neat hair, so I thought I should cut mine, too. I'd been growing it for years now, and it was long enough to come down to my chest when it was pulled straight. I asked Dan if he would do it for me. He shaved his head and had the clippers to do it, and he was surprised when I asked and even double-checked – 'Are you sure?'

But I was determined, so we gathered around in the room, and ceremoniously began to shave my head.

Once again it felt liberating, and another significant step towards saying goodbye to my old self; towards embracing my new life in friendship with Jesus.

That same evening, we met up for a Bible study, and the discussion about baptism came up. I was told that the Bible says you need to be baptised when you choose to follow Jesus. I was so excited. I was never baptised or christened as a child, and I often felt inferior when it came up in conversation. Now here was a chance to take yet another step forward.

I asked my new friends if they would baptise me, and they said they would. That was when the idea of a Christmas baptism came up. After all, it was only a few days away. We all agreed. We'd have a baptism at the flat. What more amazing way to mark the transformation in my life and the beginning of my new friendship with Jesus, than to be baptised at the time we celebrate His birthday?

15

Underwater
(Switchfoot)

OVER THE NEXT COUPLE OF DAYS, I continued exploring what had happened to me, and I spent a lot of time praying, chatting to people and discovering a real desire to read the Bible. I'd never paid any attention to it before, and I found there were so many stories of what Jesus had done, and about what His disciples did, too. I was fascinated; captivated. I wanted to be like those followers and do the things I was reading about.

How come I'd never been told all this before? It felt as though I'd missed out on it for so long, and I just had to know more and more. I spent hours at a time reading through the Gospels, simply poring over the Scriptures.

With Christmas almost here, and knowing my family were coming down from Derby, I started to sort out some presents for them all. We had arranged to meet up at Nan's house on Christmas Day for a family get-together. Everyone would be there

– Mum, Ian, Dad, Amanda (his partner), my brother and sisters, all of them. I remember sitting in my flat, bubbling and so excited to be able to tell them, face to face, what had happened to me.

The day came, and my parents, Simon and Fiona arrived to give me a lift to Nan's. They were somewhat amazed at the transformation in me, most obviously my appearance. I was no longer the bearded, hairy, pierced druggy they were used to. I was clean, with a shaved head and fresh clothes – a bit like Neo in the *Matrix* movies when he first wakes up on the Nebuchadnezzar! I was really hoping they would be so amazed by the difference that they'd know immediately it was because God is real. I've got to say, I was a little frustrated that they didn't fall to the ground and give their lives to Jesus then and there! How could they not see what had happened and that God was the reason for it?

To be honest, looking back I can't really imagine what they must have thought, but it would have been a huge shock to them.

We spent some time together at the flat, chatting, and I explained everything that had been going on. I also told them I was being baptised that evening, and gave them a few gifts.

I even returned a pocketknife to my brother that I'd stolen from him years ago. It was a gift from our dad. He was gutted when he thought he'd lost it, but I'd had it all the time. My brother was gobsmacked, I guess for two reasons: one, that I'd stolen it in the first place, and two, that I was giving it back to him.

After that, we made our way over to Nan's house, a few miles away.

It was an interesting time to say the least, all of us sitting there in the same room. I was facing my family for the first time en masse since I'd met Jesus. I was looking different; I wasn't smoking or swearing; and I wasn't high. Instead, I was talking about God, and being quizzed from all directions. I think it must have been a real brain bender for them. I remember Dad was freaked. I think they all were, but I assured them I was fine. I hadn't been drawn into some crazy cult. I'd just met God.

Of course, we did do some of the normal Christmassy stuff, too, and we ate together, but my mind was on other things. I was more excited about getting baptised that evening.

After a few hours, it was time to leave. I needed to be back at the flat. Mum, Ian, Simon and Fiona drove me into Bristol and dropped me off. As it turned out, that was the last time we were ever to be together in one place like that – as a family. Our lives soon started taking us in all different directions.

I enjoyed that time driving into town with my family. We chatted more about what I was doing and, as we arrived at the flat and I got out of the car, I just said to them, possibly for the first time in years, 'I love you all and see you soon.'

With that, they watched me walk up the steps to the front door and, no doubt with a mix of emotions, drove away.

I let myself into the flat and waited for the rest of the guys to arrive. Before long they started to appear and we began worshipping and praying together. Then we gathered in the bathroom. The bath had been filled and I climbed in and knelt down. With that, they said the words, 'We baptise you in the name of the Father, Son, and Holy Spirit ...' – and Big Pete dunked me into the tub.

They had to push me under for the full immersion. I was kneeling and I bent over backwards. As I came up out of the water, I still had my eyes shut, and the others were singing and celebrating with me.

I was praying, taking in the moment, when I saw a flash of white, then black, then white, then again black … and then I opened my eyes.

Nothing would ever be the same again. And this day was a day I would never forget.

The week after my baptism, I continued on my journey of transformation. I was hungry to learn more about the Bible and God, and I loved telling people what God had done for me. It was such an exciting time.

Even some of my old mates were asking questions, and I would try and explain to them what had happened. Others kept a very wary distance, saying, 'Marshall's got religion,' or things like that. But I wasn't a bit bothered. I knew that God had stepped into my life and that was all that mattered to me. I was making new friends now, and my life was taking new turns.

I do sometimes wonder why things went the way they did – why my friends didn't get saved, too – but I know that God was in this and had done it all for a reason. I guess I had to have some distance between me and my old lifestyle for a time.

When I decided I would sell all my records and CDs, there was no going back. I knew I wasn't going to listen to them any more. Most of the music I'd enjoyed before was dark and depressing, so I packed them up and took them to the local record shop to see what they were worth. The man at the counter offered me about £100 for the lot, which didn't seem like much, but I was just pleased to get rid of them.

Later on, as I spoke with my new friends, I decided I was going to throw a party for New Year with the money I'd got for my records. I don't know why, it just seemed like a good idea to celebrate what God had been doing. I invited them all to come along and I was so happy to share whatever I had with them. After all, they'd been instrumental in introducing me to Jesus. It was a way to say thank you.

New Year's Eve came round, and the party got under way. Several of the guys turned up with guitars and a whole host of people showed up. Some I knew, some I didn't. We had an amazing night. It wasn't the average New Year's Eve celebration, though. We sang songs, read the Bible, worshipped God and prayed together. We were all so excited, and what we were doing seemed the most natural thing in the world. There was such a tangible presence of the Holy Spirit there. Everyone was simply full of joy.

Even more amazing, that night someone else asked Jesus into their life, and the place felt electric with the presence of God. People were singing in tongues, being filled with the Holy Spirit and praying for each other all over the flat. It was an unbelievable time.

The New Year began, and I was introduced to a local pastor. He welcomed me into his church and encouraged me to learn, to listen and to pray. It was a totally different world to the one I'd been used to. These people were so kind and welcoming, and I was soon attending church regularly.

I was already aware that God was talking to me. I'd come to recognise His voice in those early days of my relationship with Him. I soon learned that this is what the Bible calls 'words of knowledge'.

I also discovered that Jesus can heal people, if we only pray. The pastor of the church had prayed for my knees, which were still causing me pain since my weight lifting days, and they had been healed instantly! As he prayed, I felt a heat on them, and then the pain subsided. I was soon fully expecting God to do more.

My first experience of God healing *through* me, was at a meeting one Sunday evening in Bristol. There was a lady there who had tennis elbow and couldn't move her arm properly. She was in considerable pain.

Whilst she was telling me about this, I figured, 'Well, I've read about this, and I've seen others do it – so I'll pray for you.'

It was really that simple, and I did it more instinctively than through any planned action. I simply placed my hand on her arm and said, 'In the name of Jesus, be healed.' It was something along those lines anyway … and instantly the lady *was* healed! She could move her arm normally. No more pain.

I fell to the floor at that moment. There was such a rush of the power of God through me, and I was in such awe that He would use me to heal someone. I watched as this lady moved her arm around. It just blew my mind.

Ever since then, I have often prayed for people to be healed. Some have been and some haven't. But even those who weren't I'm convinced experienced the presence of God.

16

Angels
(Robbie Williams)

SOME TIME DURING THOSE FIRST FEW WEEKS of my new life, I was reading through some passages in the Old Testament, and I came across the verses in Exodus chapter 21 about the freeing of Hebrew slaves:

'But if the servant declares, "I love my master and my wife and children and do not want to go free," then his master must take him before the judges. He shall take him to the door or the doorpost and pierce his ear with an awl. Then he will be his servant for life.'

As I read this passage, I felt a resonance within me. I wanted to serve God all my life. He had done something so significant in me. I knew I could never repay Him but I wanted to mark the fact, so I looked through my old earrings, and found one that was small and silver. I prayed and placed it in my ear as a symbol of my desire to serve God.

I've worn an earring in my left ear ever since that day – and many years later, it came to have huge significance.

From the moment of putting on that earring, everything changed even more. Time started flying by. I was trying to decide what I was to do with my life. I knew instantly that I wanted to tell people about what had happened to me, and some friends who were praying with me felt very clearly that I would be used as an evangelist. I was also so hungry to learn more. I became like a sponge, reading my Bible, praying, meeting people, going to church. But I was still signing on the dole, and it was then that a friend encouraged me to start looking for work.

At first, I was a bit anxious about it. After all, I hadn't worked for a good few years, and didn't have many skills to draw on. However, I felt the challenge and knew I needed to earn my keep honestly, so I started looking. Nothing really appealed to me until one of the church leaders suggested that, whilst I was looking, I could do some volunteer work.

Through a few friends, I met with some guys who were working at a Christian drop-in coffee shop on City Road in Bristol. It went by the name of 'The Missing Peace'. Here they worked with the homeless, prostitutes and addicts, providing cheap food, shelter and hot drinks for those who needed it. It was an amazing resource for the community and I agreed to help out there.

During this short time, I learned two enormously powerful lessons, and they've stayed with me ever since: I discovered the power of prayer, and the need for God's protection.

Every day we would start by praying as a team. There were usually four or five of us, serving drinks and cooking. Sometimes it was a question of just chatting with the customers. Most days things would be busy and, at times, tough, working with some of the most broken people Bristol had to offer – heroin addicts and prostitutes – but somehow we'd all manage to get through it, and do our best to show kindness and love to these needy people as they came and went.

However, one day we were all so busy getting ready, and some of the team were running late, that we didn't stop to pray. We just got things sorted out and tidied, and then we opened up.

That was the day it felt as if all hell had broken loose.

Customers were difficult, threatening, moody, aggressive, even violent. The staff were completely on edge and nothing seemed to go right. It was hard enough on a *good* day working with these hurting people and all their problems and baggage, and the demonic powers they brought in with them. But this day, it was *bad*. Everything felt so tense.

What I came to realise was just how much protection and strength we have when we invite God into our daily actions. I would often picture angels standing at the doors, keeping the powers of darkness at bay. The presence of God and the power of prayer really carries with it such a different dynamic. He truly does bring peace! By the end of that day without prayer, it felt as though we'd done ten rounds!

I never forgot that: even in the simple things, pray – always pray.

It was during my time at The Missing Peace that I started to develop my skills in leading worship. Often, on a Thursday evening after work, there would be a small gathering to worship and pray. Many of the customers would join us and I was asked to play some songs. At first I was very nervous. I'd been learning some songs, but I wasn't used to playing in front of people. In fact, the previous time I'd tried it, I was so nervous I felt sick and I shook almost uncontrollably. That said, I managed to get through it, and soon found I could use my musical skills to serve people.

After a while of working on sorting my life out, the summer of 1995 rolled round, and I read a book called *No Compromise: The Life Story of Keith Green*. He was a musician who, after meeting Jesus, devoted his life to song writing and ministry. I felt as though I wanted to do something similar. I knew from the first day I'd met Jesus that I would end up serving Him somehow, but I just couldn't figure out the way to do it. Keith Green's story inspired me.

I had been reading this book while away at a festival for a few days. On my return, I had a phone message from Mum about a college course in the Midlands, and I rang her to find out more. She'd seen an advert for a course where self-taught musicians could learn how to teach. She thought I'd do well and suggested I give it a shot and, feeling excited, I gave the college a call.

They were keen for me to apply and told me I had to send in a demo, which I happily did. A few days later, they got back in touch with me telling me they'd accepted my application and would be happy for me to join the course – 'Oh, and by the way, it starts on Monday.'

That didn't give me a lot of time – I think the day they contacted me was Thursday!

I had some thinking to do. Should I go for it? Should I put it off? What about the flat? More importantly, what about church?

I rang Mum, told her they'd accepted me and that I needed to start on Monday. We agreed that, if I decided to go for it, I could stay at her house, which at least made the idea of a move a little easier.

So, I literally grabbed everything I needed, made a few calls and that was it. I was out of Bristol. The next thing I knew, I was on my way to Derby to start a new life there, with nothing more than a bag and a guitar.

In hindsight, I realise I didn't go about all this in a very neat and tidy fashion. I just abandoned the flat, left behind everything I didn't need and set off for Derby. Apparently, so my uncle told me, when he arrived at the flat to check on things one day, it was like walking aboard the Marie Celeste – everything was still there, except me!

17

The Riverflow
(The Levellers)

MY TIME IN DERBY WAS A MIXED BAG TO START WITH. Living with Mum and Ian again was by no means easy. There was a whole host of emotions to deal with, as well as some old hurts and some new frustrations to work through, and having to learn to share the space with my younger brother and sister proved entertaining at times, too.

Then there was the fact that none of my family believed in Jesus.

I'd been pretty much used to coping by myself (albeit badly) and doing my own thing since I was 17, and now I was back under my family's roof. I couldn't help feeling isolated and a bit trapped not knowing any Christians locally.

And then, of course, my family had to get used to having me around again!

There were moments when my frustration would get the better of me, and we'd have some pretty heated discussions around the dinner table. Though that time wasn't easy, I can see that it really was a part of God's plan to bring some healing back into my family, and it wasn't long before He built some new connections and things started to settle down.

I'd been looking for a church to go to locally but, as yet, it was proving to be a fruitless exercise. Nothing really seemed to fit. However, after ringing some friends in Bristol and asking them to pray, they came back to me with some good news. They'd just been to a conference where they'd met a guy from Derby. He was part of a local church and just happened to live about five minutes away from Mum's house.

I couldn't believe my ears. I'd been in Derby for a while now and was just starting to get despondent. The timing was perfect. We met up, and before long he had introduced me to the church he belonged to. I was quickly accepted there and made to feel welcome. The very first day I went along to one of their public meetings, I was given a prophecy all about music, rhythm and creativity. It was a real confirmation.

That church in Derby was very kind and generous and supported me all the way through college. Also, knowing I was finding it tough trying to live at home again, one of the guys there offered me a spare room in his house.

What a Godsend that room was. When I wasn't at college or working, I had the house to myself during the day, and I really enjoyed the freedom I had to pray and spend time with God. That just wasn't so easy living at Mum's. Now I felt I could stretch my wings again, and would spend literally hours just hanging out with God, then shooting off to college or over the road to the pub where I had landed a job working behind the bar.

It wasn't long before I got quite involved in the life of the church, too. There was to be a church plant just up the road from where I was living (this is where a new Christian church is set up) and, being musical, I had some great opportunities to lead worship and learn more about the process of church planting in its early stages. There were some smaller cell groups that I was part of, too, and it all brought a richness to my life.

Once I'd completed the college course with good grades, I quickly found myself teaching guitar for a living. Alongside that, I was still working part-time in the pub. But I knew there was more of significance that I could be doing. For the time being, though, I decided to go with the flow.

About a year after college, the church offered to send me on a training year that went by the name of 'TiE teams'. I would be based in Derby, working for the church, but would also be getting some teaching and input from a broad spectrum of Christian leaders across the UK.

TiE teams (Training in Evangelism), now known as 'dna', do pretty much exactly what the name says. To be honest, when I first thought of getting involved, the thought terrified me. I almost ran a mile when I realised I would be expected to take part in street work, youth work, schools, clubs, assemblies and children's work. However, after praying and wrestling with the idea, I soon realised that it was part of God's agenda for my life. So, yet again, in a very short space of time, I jumped on a train, went to an interview and got accepted. I would start in just a few weeks.

What a time that turned out to be, autumn 1996 to summer 1997. God blew my mind!

I loved TiE teams. During that year, whilst working with a couple called Doug and Belinda Horley at Spring Harvest, I learned about God's heart for children. I was overwhelmed with excitement, and I soon wanted to learn more.

To start with, I wasn't looking forward to Spring Harvest at all. In fact, if I'm honest, I couldn't think of anything worse. I wasn't a children's worker, and I really dragged my heels getting the paperwork done for the event.

However, once I was there, I instantly made friends with a whole host of other young Christians, and thoroughly enjoyed myself. Doug and the team led the events from the stage and we were out amongst the kids. I'd never been to anything like this before. There were 800 or so kids in one place, all being taught about God and experiencing His presence and power.

That year, there were kids healed of all kinds of complaints – one little boy had a deaf ear that just 'popped' open after we'd been praying!

I also learned about living by faith. I had to raise money for TiE teams, and I soon realised that God is totally reliable. I discovered so much more about the Bible, too, about the history of the Church, and almost every subject in between. And I had space to develop my musical gifting. Some of the amazing people I met there I'm still friends with today.

Towards the summer of that year, because of some of the connections I had made at Spring Harvest, I was invited to work for a church in Epsom as a youth, children's and schools' worker, and continue my training there. I was also very keen to learn more from Doug Horley so, as he was part of the church I was invited to, it all seemed to be falling into place. I prayed about it and it felt as though God was in the move, so I accepted the invitation, and in September 1997, I moved to Epsom. I have been here ever since.

I have to say that it all sounds rosy up to this point and, on the whole, things were pretty good. I was learning more and more about hearing from God. I'd have dreams, receive words of knowledge, and I'd prophesy. I was learning about people, church and myself. Of course, I made some goofs along the way – mostly where I'd end up making rash decisions that upset a few people (completely unintentionally, mind you, and I've subsequently endeavoured to put things right). Fortunately, on the whole, I was shown much grace.

Compared to what was to come, however, most of these little blunders just paled into insignificance.

In 1996, Martin Smith, from the band Delirious?, wrote a song called *History Maker*, which has been a continuing inspiration to me. There have been times when I've literally felt as though these were words from the heart of God right to mine. I heard it for the first time in Derby, and I loved it. It was this song, along with many others, that was to keep me pressing forwards, even when times were tough.

Is it true today that when people pray
Cloudless skies will break,
Kings and queens will shake?
Yes, it's true, and I believe it,
I'm living for You.

Is it true today that when people pray
We'll see dead men rise,
And the blind set free?
Yes, it's true, and I believe it,
I'm living for You.

I'm gonna be a history maker in this land.
I'm gonna be a speaker of truth to all mankind.
I'm gonna stand, I'm gonna run into Your arms,
Into Your arms again,
Into Your arms,
Into Your arms again.

Yes it's true today that when people stand
With the fire of God and the truth in hand,
We'll see miracles, we'll see angels sing,
We'll see broken hearts making history.
Yes, it's true, and I believe it.
I'm living for You.

Something in the words captured my attention. I believe in a mighty God of love, grace and awesome power; a God who takes the weak things of the world to shame the wise; a God who loves so unconditionally, that to grasp Him will take more than a lifetime.

Yet because of what Jesus did for us, we can have free access to the God of creation. Even as I write, I'm listening to Martin Smith's song, and it reduces me to tears. My heart rings with the melody of heaven.

I want to be a History Maker; I want to be a speaker of truth to all mankind.

I believe God wants to raise up history makers, men, women and children who will take hold of the truth of Jesus Christ and run with it throughout the whole world, making disciples, healing the sick, casting out demons, performing signs and wonders, simply because they are not afraid to give in. They are not ashamed of the Gospel – not afraid to say 'yes' to God and 'no' to the world. They refuse to give in to the devil and his deceit.

I believe God wants me to be one of those people. I was a broken and weak man, and yet God, in His kindness, uses me. He speaks through me to others, not because of my skills or my gifting, but because He loves me so much. He wants us to work with Him, bringing redemption to the entire world, in the name of Jesus. I'd rather do that than anything else! Do I look foolish? Does this sound childlike?

Or does it sound like the way the Kingdom works?

The song, *History Maker*, and many others written by Martin Smith, have kept me going through the dark times. I believe God planted this song and vision in me to hold me through the years to come.

18

Black Dog
(Led Zeppelin)

I'D BEEN LIVING IN EPSOM for about six months. I was working for Generation Church doing all kinds of things, from school assemblies to lessons that covered issues ranging from the media to drugs awareness. I was settling in and making friends and was also meeting regularly with some guys on the second year of TiE teams. A friend had offered me a room to live in whilst I was still training and I'd found a part-time job at a local sports shop. I even had a girlfriend for the first time in nearly four years. Things were looking good.

However, with all the pressure of moving, two new jobs, training, a new church, new friendships, and a girlfriend, what seemed like a relatively normal, if exciting, existence, soon started to reveal that there were some issues from my past remaining unresolved. I was trying to fit in and be the good 'Christian' that I thought was expected of me, but I seemed to be feeling a huge amount of pressure to conform.

I was having a hard time trying to work within a frustrating framework, and I just couldn't maintain it. I was beginning to feel boxed in and under pressure from all sides. I'd moved to a new area which had very different value systems from what I'd been used to, and I've often felt there is a spiritual oppression hanging over the place, too. I realise now I was like a fish out of water. Finding it hard to keep up the pace, I was hurting, and years of childhood rejection and pain were starting to come to the surface. A fog seemed to descend on me. My head felt as if it was wrapped in a duvet most of the time. I was numb.

It seemed to be almost impossible for me to make decisions or to stay focused, and it was becoming so hard just to get out of bed. Even the closeness I had always experienced with God seemed to be ebbing away. I was starting to feel lost, alone, angry and frustrated.

Then, around May 1998, I just hit a wall. I remember sitting in the Generation Church office, chatting with the church leader, and as we spoke she suggested that maybe I was suffering from depression. Perhaps I should go and see a doctor.

What a blow. I felt like a complete failure. I had experienced the power of God in my life in a more dynamic way than many of the people I'd been meeting. I had seen so many healings and I was hungry to serve God and do His will – and yet I'd got to the point where I couldn't even decide what shoes to wear, or what meal to eat. Everything was crumbling around my ears.

Black dog had come to visit. (Black dog is what Sir Winston Churchill nick-named depression. It's a good summing up – a seemingly invisible black cloud just turns up like a stray dog and, uninvited, makes camp in your life.) It was to be a very long time before I was free from the clutches of this illness.

I arranged to visit the doctor; he asked me a list of questions, and came to the conclusion, yep, you're depressed … But don't worry, lots of people are. He prescribed some medication for the condition, signed me off work for a month and put me in touch with a psychotherapist.

I was bummed out. I had to speak to the church and to the sports shop. I had to tell everyone I knew, 'Really sorry, folks, I'm depressed. Can't do anything. Doctor's signed me off.' I had to deal with the fact that I wasn't coping. I was broken, and on top of that was the disappointment that God hadn't sorted this stuff out. With all the miraculous intervention in my life so far, He somehow hadn't worked out this little problem. I had to take anti-depressant drugs to be able to get by.

It was a total wipe-out. What? Why? How?

I had so many questions, but very few answers.

Over the next few years, I found myself in and out of counselling, and on and off the medication. What I came to realise during that time was that, even though God had stepped into my life and had made a huge impact in the areas of addiction and all the things I really couldn't do for myself, there were a load of emotional and psychological issues that simply needed working through. I had so much anger to process in order to make me whole again, and there's no short cut for that, really. My thinking needed readjusting and I had to have help doing that.

It was hard at first to come to terms with the fact that I needed medication, especially when so many of my previous problems had been drug related. I was scared of ending up addicted to these tablets, too. But with some wise council, I came to see that my thinking and emotions were broken, which is what had led to some of the depression. In the same way that if you break your leg you need a plaster cast to help it heal, so, for now, I needed the medication. It was like a plaster cast for my emotions. I submitted myself to the process and clung on to God with every ounce of faith and hope that I had.

Baring your soul to other people is no easy task, either. There were things in my past I had never spoken of to anyone – things I had done, things that had been done to me, things I'd felt and hidden. There was simply so much pain because of the rejection I'd been carrying around for so long. There were attitudes and thought processes there which I'd learned as coping mechanisms as a child, though I'd never consciously adopted them. Clearly they weren't working in my life now as an adult and really needed to change.

It was time for some renewing of my mind, just like the apostle Paul wrote about in his letter to the Romans. Even though this would be a difficult time, I was prepared to do it if God would only give me the strength to hold on.

There were moments during those years when I felt I really couldn't deal with it. It was too difficult. I'd known the closeness of God … but not any more.

By now I'd split up with my girlfriend. In retrospect, I realise that, even at the very start of this relationship, it was not part of God's plan for me. I felt Him say it wouldn't go anywhere because of my insecurities. But my need to be wanted and loved, coupled with the desire I had to be married, were emotions with a stronger hold on me than my ability to walk in obedience to God. I tried all I could to maintain the relationship, but I couldn't shake the feeling it just wasn't going anywhere. Things weren't right between us, and eventually I knew it had to end.

That was a hard lesson learned. I realised I had been disobedient to God, and the result was a tempestuous relationship which left both parties hurting. Had I been wiser, it would never had happened.

When it was over, I figured I'd better just get things sorted with God. I felt I had to lay down my right to be in a relationship. I'd always had an eye for women, but some time later, during a 24/7 prayer week, I told God that I surrendered my right to be married and I'd give my life totally to Him. I sobbed my heart out, sitting in a cold van that was turned into a prayer room, but in that moment, I knew I had completely given over my will to His.

That day I started to learn to surrender; to let go and trust God with everything. If He was ever to bring anyone into my life, that was up to Him. To all intents and purposes, however, I was at last beginning to learn how to die to myself. I was prepared to be single for the rest of my life and serve Him.

Around this time, I also moved house. I was still doing some church work and occasionally leading worship, but mainly I was teaching guitar and just doing my best trying to hang in there. I was feeling lonely and isolated, and was coming awfully close to the end of my tether. The depression was still over me and there seemed to be no light at the end of the tunnel. That fog just wouldn't seem to lift for any decent length of time.

I don't know that I could have felt much worse. I was up and down like a human yo-yo.

One time I remember sitting on my own, aching from head to foot in emotional pain, wishing God would take me away right now. And as I was praying and wrestling with Him, I realised there really was nowhere for me to go. It was either hold on – or kill myself. I found great strength in the verse in the Bible where Jesus' disciples say, 'We've left everything to follow you.' That's how I felt. I really had given everything to follow Jesus, and there was only one solution: hold on. Just keep going.

I knew God had touched my life. I knew He had a purpose for me and I couldn't simply forget all that He had done. I still loved Him, even though I found it so difficult to connect with Him just now. I had to believe that He could bring me through all this. I had to believe that God could break in and bring me freedom. If He couldn't, what kind of God was He?

I don't know that this was a turning point, but what I can see now is that it was faith at its most raw. The simple, determined faith to hang on, even though I had nothing left to give; when it felt as if God was a million miles away; when all I could do was say, 'Yes, Lord. Even if this is my lot in life, I choose to trust You and follow You. Even if for the rest of my life I'll walk with a metaphoric limp, I'll hang on.'

After all, faith isn't really faith until it's all you've got. I felt I'd been stripped to the core. I could hardly lift my head up – often I could hardly even get up – but I held on.

19

Pressing On
(Bob Dylan)

PRETTY SOON AFTER THAT, things did slowly start to change for the better. I was still on the medication and occasionally seeing a counsellor, but my circumstances were starting to look a little brighter.

I had started a college course in Guildford at the Academy of Contemporary Music, where I was working hard at developing my skills as a guitarist. It was a great year. I got to play guitar every day for fun and met some really cool people. My confidence grew and I started to make some good friends. Yet again, God provided me with the finances I needed to fund the course.

It was around this time that I started to spend some time with a lovely girl called Dawn. She seemed to take a real shine to me. Soon we were regularly emailing and, before too long, we were seeing each other.

I remember the first time I knew I really liked her. The family I lodged with were away and Dawn came to visit. She just popped in for a cuppa and we ended up spending the whole day together. We ordered pizza and hung out. It was such a lovely time, and the very beginnings of a new future together. Dawn has played such a huge role in bringing healing to my life, and even though I was prepared to go it solo for the rest of my days, God knew we would be great for each other.

I realised that through the whole process of letting go of my desires, freedom had come. When Dawn and I finally connected, it was driven by healthy motives rather than the insecurities that drove previous relationships.

The whole area of dying to self has been a constant challenge throughout my Christian walk, and I'm sure it will continue to be so. But I've come to realise that it really is the only way we can live in fullness with God. Jesus Himself said, 'For whoever wants to save his life will lose it, but whoever loses his life for me will find it.' I had to discover that, to allow God to be Lord of my life, I needed to learn to submit that life to His will. This ultimately meant dying to *my* agendas and *my* dreams, and allowing Him to lead me wherever He wanted to.

Consequently, He has now blessed me with a wife and three wonderful children – and many of the values that I used to hold dear no longer seem important.

Around Christmas 2001, I introduced my dad to Dawn. We went down to visit him and his partner and I felt it was a significant step for me. I had always lived under the desperate need for his approval, and whenever we saw each other, he would comment that he thought I should have stayed together with an ex-girlfriend, and couldn't understand why we had split up. I'm sure much of the tension I felt in my previous relationship was because of this need for him to approve.

For me to introduce him to the woman I was planning to propose to was by no means an easy process. It felt I was finally making my own choices as an adult – whether he approved or not, that was the way it was going to be. In fact, I wasn't even seeking his approval any more.

As it turned out, he did approve. It's hard not to like Dawn. She's so gentle, patient and kind. We had a lovely time with my dad and Amanda that day. It was a real turning point for me.

Then came Christmas Day 2001, and Dawn and I had gone to visit my family in Derby. We had driven up on Christmas Eve from Epsom. I was slightly nervous. I was planning to propose to Dawn the next day, but she had no idea.

The morning came and I asked her to marry me. I'd made her a stocking of presents and at the bottom was a ring box, containing a diamond engagement ring and a message.

Dawn said yes.

We had a wonderful day and we planned for a short engagement, as we weren't interested in an expensive or elaborate wedding. We just wanted to get on with being together, and to celebrate with our family and friends. When we got home from Derby, we set a date – 30th March 2002, during the Easter holidays while I was on a break from college.

At the beginning of February, I got a phone call from my brother, Simon. Dad's partner was in hospital in Southampton after having some health problems and Dad was expected to be there to visit, but no one had seen or heard from him. Amanda was worried, so one of Dad's friends had been to the house to see if he was all right, but couldn't get an answer.

Eventually the police had been called and they broke into the house, only to find that Dad had died of a massive stroke during the night. My brother was the only contact number they could find among his possessions.

I rushed down to see Amanda. It was such a shock. That Christmas just passed turned out to be the last time I'd see him alive. He was only 54.

Dad had died and I was completely gutted. His death left me with such a mixed bag of emotions after all the years of pain and rejection. Yet for me there was also a strange sense of freedom: I would no longer suffer from those feelings of rejection.

There was a huge sense of shock and grief, of course, but perhaps more over the dad that could have been, especially as I felt we might now have got to know each other on a new footing.

With all this going on, I could sense the clouds of depression looming over me again. Somehow, though, with God's grace and the wedding to look forward too, this time I did manage to keep them from swallowing me. Knowing that I would soon be getting married and starting a new life with Dawn offered a great ray of hope for the future.

Dad's funeral was certainly a tough day. Amanda made all the arrangements. Although she'd been really sick herself, she managed to sort things the way she wanted. My brother, myself and my uncle, together with some of Dad's closest friends, carried the coffin into the little church on the south coast. For all his faults, my father was a very popular guy and the place was packed. People I'd known from childhood right down to new friends he'd made more recently, they all came to pay their respects – even Mum and Ian were there from Derby. There were many tears that day, yet I think there was the beginning of some healing, too – especially for Mum and us kids.

Despite everything, we still decided to go ahead with our wedding. On 30th March, exactly as planned, Dawn and I were married.

I couldn't wait! I remember standing at the front of the church hall, no nerves, just excitement. I wore the gold earring that Dad had had made for him from my grandmother's wedding ring. It was handed to me as a sign of remembrance, but I soon took it out again as continuing to wear it somehow didn't feel right. I placed it in a drawer to be forgotten for the next few years.

Dawn looked amazing and smiled from ear to ear as she walked down the aisle. We were surrounded by all our friends and family, except Amanda who was too ill to come along. We worshipped and had such a lively service. Many people who came along were amazed at the fun and joy that surrounded our wedding – it was the first time some of them had been to a ceremony like that that wasn't stuffy or religious.

Our good friend, Doug Horley, took the service, and Dawn and I enjoyed every single minute of it. Later we celebrated at a local sports centre that had been decorated for the event by church friends. It was the only place large enough to fit in everyone we wanted to be there!

We spent our first night together at a local hotel before jetting off for an amazing honeymoon in Texas. Thanks to some very generous friends, we had the run of their house, with a pool, and a Jacuzzi outside our bedroom door. They even loaned us a convertible Porsche while we were there. It was a much needed break and we loved our first weeks together. It was so good just to get away and spend time with each other after everything that had been going on. We ate, drank, shopped, and really chilled out. It was great.

When we arrived back in the UK, Dawn and I started to make our little flat a home, and I returned to continue my college course. That summer, I graduated. I didn't quite get the grades I'd been hoping for, but considering everything that had been happening I was just pleased to have graduated at all. I started teaching guitar again and looked for jobs as a session musician.

April 2004 saw the birth of our first Daughter, Skyla. Dawn's waters broke very early, at around only 32 weeks, so she had to spend nearly four weeks in hospital. I was on edge the whole time, never knowing when the baby would appear. Eventually, after a tough labour, there she was, premature but healthy.

This little girl had such a huge impact on me; this tiny little bundle of life, utterly helpless and vulnerable, yet so beautiful. Skyla unlocked something in me that I didn't even know was there. She's such a pretty girl, sensitive and caring, and now loves to sing and dance.

After she was born, I really started to learn to love on a deeper level than I ever realised was possible. I started to see how God sees. Loving unconditionally, He's the Father I always needed and I had to become a father to begin to understand Him.

With Skyla's birth, I started to feel God's call to my heart again – and soon I had plans to evangelise the whole world!

In January 2006, my second daughter, Keira, arrived. After yet another tough labour, out she came, screaming at the top of her lungs. It was such a high pitched sound that people thought she was in pain.

She wasn't. Keira continued screaming whenever we were out, or in the car, or at home … She made sure she wasn't going be ignored. She is such a bundle of fun, always up to mischief, or climbing things or jumping off things. And always laughing.

In the last few months, Dawn and I have been blessed with a third beautiful daughter, Neave Hope. Together, these three kids have brought such a healing to my life. They've been instrumental in God's process of restoration.

I've got to say that I sometimes find it hard to believe I've been so rewarded. My life was never going this way. In fact, if it weren't for meeting Jesus, I honestly don't think I'd be writing this book. I don't think I'd even be alive. I'm convinced I would have overdosed or committed suicide in a fit of depression. Even Amanda once said that, if it wasn't for God, she's sure I would have killed myself the way my life was going.

Such grace I have been shown!

20

Burn Away
(Foo Fighters)

IT WAS WITH THE BIRTH OF SKYLA that God started to do even more work in me. I felt compelled to share the love I was feeling for Him, and was soon on a path to a new project – 3st (Thirst).

It made sense to me to combine my musical skills with my passion for communicating the Gospel, so an evangelistic rock band was born. I had a vision to see it perform in schools and for youth groups, which would create a platform to preach the Gospel. Three of us formed the band, and it wasn't too long before we started writing and gigging.

For about two years, we had some great times, playing in local schools and really feeling the presence of the Holy Spirit. We even started a local youth event for young people to come along to and worship and engage with God.

God began to put a vision in my heart of raising up an army

of youth who would carry the Gospel message and be completely on fire for God. I could see thousands of people in these visions, but yet again I was to learn that my dreams were going to have to die, as God took what I had to offer and, over time, reshaped it into what I am today. I had to learn that my desire to do some of these things was more about me and my ego than about God and spreading His Word.

God began refining and transforming the vision, and eventually (perhaps somewhat inevitably) the band fell by the wayside. I was feeling under pressure from the church leadership to perform and get everything right, and that started to interfere with my relationship with the other band members. My drummer and best friend, in particular, didn't feel he had the same drive for the band that I had, and consequently it was putting a strain on our friendship. I was devastated, but in the end I had to let him make his own choices about it.

Letting go was really hard for me. I felt as though my heart was broken and my vision gone, but I did learn a great lesson: letting people go matters more than a vision or a dream. There is nothing more important in this world besides God than people, and loving each other as Christ loves us. Subsequently, Pete (yes, another one!) and I are still the best of mates, and I value his friendship now more than ever.

When the band finally folded, there still remained within me a strong sense of calling to preach the Gospel and follow the vision – but in a way that God saw fit, not according to *my* agenda.

I've come to realise that, over the last ten years, God has been systematically peeling away layers of hurt and pain, and the behaviour patterns that have hindered my walk with Him. He's been teaching me lessons that will influence the way I live for the rest of my life, and He continues to do so.

I've spent so much of my life seeking the approval of man, and always feeling as if I needed someone to do the job with me, whatever it might be. I haven't wanted to be a lone ranger. Now I can see that I can't allow my need of others to stop me doing what God has asked me to do. He's challenged me time and time again to step out, and when I've done so, others have joined with me. My first source of approval has to come from God. If I, or any of us, look to other places, we will live constantly with guilt, failure, rejection, disappointment and shame, especially when it comes to matters of faith. When others can't see what you see, you simply have to step out of the boat and see what happens. God has shown me that living life any other way isn't healthy.

Dawn and I have been taught about money and how to be good stewards of what God has given us. On an even deeper level, He's called us to challenge the consumerist mindset of our society, to live within our means and to realise that everything we have is His. We needed to surrender everything to Him – after all, we're simply looking after it for Him – and in so doing, He has demonstrated His absolute faithfulness in providing for us and meeting our needs.

And we can do nothing to earn His love or favour, other than simply receive it with gratitude.

God has also spoken to us time and time again about His belief in us. It's not all about our faith in Him. God believes in us, too, the body of Christ – His people – to complete the mission He has given us. Though He doesn't need us, He chooses to use us, and if we will only learn to surrender our desire for control and power, He'll do some of the most amazing things we will ever see.

I've come to see that the only way to live in this world is God's way, and I, for one, am pursuing Jesus with all my heart, all my energy, and all my life. I'm not interested in religion, or the trappings that surround our faith. I want to walk in the fullness of God's purposes for me and my family. And I want everyone I know to realise that freedom, too.

I want to be known as a friend of Jesus.

*   *   *   *   *

A leap forward to 2008, and my return home from Spring Harvest following an extraordinary dream, where this telling of my story began. What a staggering year that was!

I travelled half-way round the world to work with children in Kyrgyzstan (Central Asia). I had the opportunity to speak to hundreds of people and watched as God broke through into their lives, refreshing many and healing others. It was a privilege to be a part of what He was doing.

God put a fresh desire in my heart that year for evangelism, for mission, for prayer, for intimacy with Him and for the prophetic gifting. There was a growing passion in my heart to follow Jesus no matter what the cost; to go into the world and make disciples; to love mercy and justice, and to be an agent for change in a world that desperately needs it.

When Spring Harvest was over, I arrived home searching for more of God. I was hungrier than I've ever been to know what He wanted of me. I started praying and fasting, earnestly seeking Him.

That's when I found my dad's old gold earring (the one he'd had made from his grandmother's wedding ring) in the drawer next to my desk, and I felt it was time I did something with it.

Because I didn't feel as though it was quite right for me, I asked a silversmith friend of mine if she would reshape it for me. It felt symbolic of what God had been doing in my life over the last few years, healing and reshaping me, making me what He wants me to be. I am no longer just a child of my earthly father, but I am a child of my heavenly Father, and have been re-made.

My friend agreed to work on it for me, and said she would pray whilst doing it, so I left it with her.

One night during May, I turned on the TV and flicked through a few channels, eventually coming to the God Channel on cable. To my surprise, there was a tattooed preacher on, yelling in the name of Jesus and praying for healing of the sick. He instantly got my attention.

This guy was not your usual saccharin-sweet, smooth-talking TV evangelist. He was all out going for it! I wondered what was going on. Since the band had folded, God had slowly been drawing the ego out of me, and I'd gone off 'platform' ministry. I couldn't see how it could be effective. But suddenly, here was this guy preaching to thousands, and clearly God was at work.

That was the night, watching that show, that God challenged me:

'Who do you think you are to limit how I work and who I work through? You can either believe or not, the choice is up to you.' Then He added, 'Are you prepared to be a fool for me, Jase?'

The next night, Dawn and I watched together as this same guy screamed and shouted. When we switched off the TV, we chatted and prayed together. At that moment, the Holy Spirit fell on the room, and I felt prompted to pray for her healing, which I did.

The next day, Dawn came into the bedroom excited and bouncing around, saying she had been healed! I was delighted. I often find myself praying for people, but recently I'd been feeling as though I had very little faith. A lot of my thoughts were cynical and negative. Yet in the past 24 hours, God had challenged me to stop putting limitations on Him. The scales seemed to have dropped from my eyes and I felt alive in my heart again. He was definitely stirring things up in me.

I've always known there is real power in the Gospel. After all I've experienced it first hand. But I've long felt that this version of Christianity that we do in the West is lacking something. It seems so preoccupied with self-preservation and comfort, and even with conforming to the power of the world rather than that of the Kingdom. Cynicism had crept into me and I seemed to have lost so much faith – or perhaps even confidence.

Over the next few nights, I watched this programme on the God Channel as the controversy started to grow around it.

Then one evening, the prophet, Bob Jones, was talking, discussing revival, and sharing some of the visions he had seen in the Spirit. Suddenly, he mentioned the verses in the Bible (Exodus 21:5-6 and Deuteronomy 15:16-17) about servants who had been set free but wanted to stay and serve their masters, so would have their ears pierced with an awl and serve them for life.

I was amazed! The verse in Exodus was the one I'd read years earlier, as a result of which I'd decided always to wear an earring, as a sign of my desire to serve God. It felt as though this guy was talking directly to me – I had just asked Claire to reshape my dad's gold earring for me. My heart was racing! I knew God was speaking.

The very next evening, as our small group met, my friend, the silversmith, arrived with the finished, reshaped earring. I shared the story of what had happened the night before, we committed the ring to God in prayer, and I put it in.

21

Now Is The Time
(Delirious?)

FROM THAT POINT ON, I have been seeking God with a renewed vigour. I have been studying, praying, reading. I have a growing sense that God is calling His people back to the heart of the Gospel. The simple truth is that Jesus is Lord over everything, from our personal, internal lives to our finances, from our time to our family, to our communities. The question is, are we prepared to allow Him to be so? Will we follow Jesus whatever the cost? Will those of us in the comfortable places of life count the cost, give all we have to the poor and follow Christ?

Are we prepared to die to self, take up our crosses and live for God?

I fully believe that, as we allow God into those places, as we let Him reshape our thinking so that we aim to build our lives on foundations of love, trust, hope, humility and servant hood, that we will truly see a massive outpouring of His power in these times.

I believe the challenges to us as 21st century Christians are to reject worldly thinking of bigger, better, more power, control and empire. We need to learn to model our lives on giving rather than receiving, and on serving rather than being served. We need to shout, 'STOP!' at this never-ending treadmill of consumerism that robs us of the time, life and energy we should have for loving one another, and reject the life of comfort we live, which, rather than bringing us peace, swallows us up.

Jesus said, 'Where your riches are, there is your heart.' Is it any wonder we are so desperate for peace when we spend most of our time consuming, acquiring and then protecting what we have?

Surely it's time to embrace the cross.

Where the Church has established 'religious' rather than relational Christianity, it's time to turn back to God. Where we make idols of the mechanism that is supposed to serve Him, which so often becomes another time, money and energy drain and leaves us feeling weary and burdened rather than fulfilled and free, we need to re-learn to pursue the heart of our Lord and Saviour, Jesus Christ, and have a heart like David (as the singer-songwriter, Kevin Prosch, once wrote).

Revival is on its way – I fully believe it – yet it will come at a cost. So many of the things we hold dear will be revealed as the idols they've become. We are given the choice: do we want idols made of wood, stone and metal, or do we want to know the heart of the Creator? Are we prepared to surrender our intellectual religion for that of a faith from the heart?

It really is time for a revolution. I don't mean one of violence or destruction, but of love, mercy, justice, kindness and selflessness. It is time to be renewed in mind and spirit, and then get on with the business of the Kingdom, and not that of Western Christendom.

I believe God is calling … Will you answer, and walk off into the desert if that's where He leads, in the hope of the Promised Land?

About five years ago, God gave me a picture.

I saw an army of men and women who had decided to look to Christ as Lord. There were hundreds, possibly thousands, marching to the beat of a different drum. Their eyes were fixed on Jesus, not concerned with 'religion', but slowly and powerfully transforming the world, changing power structures and challenging corrupt systems. Many of these people had been badly hurt, many were fatherless and rejected, but they had captured the love God has for them, and now they pressed on to change the world.

I saw the hunger in these men and women that was driving them relentlessly in search of a father's love, desperate for the affirmation that they rightfully needed. Many of these children had searched in the darkest corners for the hole in their hearts to be filled, but when they finally found the love of God, everything changed.

I saw them coming to Jesus and finding healing for the years of damage and rejection.

I saw them being transformed from the weak and broken to the strong and powerful. God, who takes the weak things of the world, would shame the wise with these people who, after such pain and loss, were captivated by the love of the Father who created them.

I saw radical, committed young men and women, who would not be stopped by anything. They had been debilitated for so long, and now they had freedom and knew the Father's all-encompassing love, they would not be bound again.

They would blaze with a desire to fulfil the Great Commission (Matthew 28). They would not be stopped. They would run harder and burn brighter than many who had gone before them. They would live the message of Jesus, taking the Sermon on the Mount seriously, and living as the disciples did in the book of Acts.

They would be marked by the love they have for one another and their willingness to embrace the cross. They would learn to die to themselves and, rejecting all the grabbing, clawing distractions of the world and its value systems, these men and women would lead a great awakening.

There is an army rising.

At Christmas in 1994, God stepped into my life and turned me around. He didn't save me just from a life of sin. He didn't die to save me *from* anything.

He died to save me *for* something – and the same is true for you, too.

Jesus Christ died for the sins of the world. Every principality and power has been overthrown; even the power of death

143

has been undone. The Lord Jesus has done everything necessary at the cross and with His resurrection two thousand years ago. The veil has been torn. We can now come boldly into the presence of God and partner with Him to make a difference in this world right now, with signs and wonders following.

And what rewards there will be for those who choose to say, 'Yes, Lord.'

The time is now.

Your time is now.